THE ENCHANTING OWL

Connie Toops
Foreword by Mike Everett

VOYAGEUR PRESS

For my father, who opened my eyes to the natural world, and my mother, who gave me the words to share what I saw.

Text copyright © 1990 by Connie Toops
Photography copyrights as noted by each photograph

Printed in Hong Kong

90 91 92 93 94 5 4 3 2 1

Library of Congress Cataloging-in-Publication data
Toops, Connie M.
    The enchanting owl / Connie Toops ; foreword by Mike Everett.
        p.   cm. — (Voyageur wilderness books)
    Includes bibliographical references (p.) and index.
    ISBN 0–89658–136–5
    ISBN 0–89658–140–3 (pbk.)
    1. Owls—North America.   2. Owls—Europe.   I. Title. II.
Series.
    QL696.S8T66 1990
    598'.97—dc20   90–12506
                                                        CIP
Published by Voyageur Press, Inc.
P.O. Box 338
123 North Second Street
Stillwater, MN 55082 U.S.A.
In Minn 612–430–2210
Toll-free 800–888–9653

Voyageur Press books are also available at discounts for bulk quantities for educational, fundraising, premium, or sales-promotion use. For details contact the marketing manager. Please write or call for our free catalog of natural history publications.

Quote on page **58** is reprinted by permission of the Smithsonian Institution Press from *The Great Gray Owl: Phantom of the Northern Forest*, by Robert W. Nero. Smithsonian Institution, Washington, D.C. 1980, p. 110.

CONTENTS

ACKNOWLEDGMENTS

I am grateful to David Hitzig of the Animal Rehabilitation Center, Tropical Audubon Society, Miami, Florida, David Livingston of Brukner Nature Center, Troy, Ohio, and the staff of Lichterman Nature Center, Memphis, Tennessee, for allowing me to observe and photograph the owls in their care. I also wish to thank Ed Clark, Terry Lindsay, Kay McKeever, Jamie Primm, and Anne Tappan for information they provided on owl rehabilitation. Finally, I wish to acknowledge the assistance of Bruce Colvin, Mike Everett, Paul Kerlinger, Robert W. Nero, Nick Riddiford, Devi Sharp, Tony Soper, and Dr. I. R. Taylor who read and offered advice on portions of this manuscript.

FOREWORD

It was the noise made by a group of crows that gave the game away. My fellow owl-freak Noble Proctor was certain about the reason for all the agitation and, sure enough, there it was — a great, barrel-shaped blob half hidden in the branches, quite motionless until, suddenly, its top portion shifted position and a big golden-rimmed eye glared down at us. A great horned owl, the first I had ever seen!

I have seen others since, but the memory of that first one remains very special. It ranks alongside other owl firsts — the long-eared owl in a Scottish sea buckthorn thicket, the eagle owl on a limestone cliff in Germany, the burrowing owl on the Kissimmee Prairie and the female snowy owl on a Shetland island, just to name a few. I am lucky to have watched, listened to, and marvelled at owls in lots of places and, like Connie Toops, I am fascinated by them. I have a soft spot for the big (it is, to a European) barred owl, and I suspect she has too. Connie doesn't say so, but I bet, like me, she wished she had coined that immortal phrase of Thoreau's: "I rejoice that there are owls." In so many ways, that says it all.

Since Europe and North America share a number of species, it is most appropriate to write about the owls of both continents. Several notable books on owls have been produced on both sides of the Atlantic in the last decade or so and *The Enchanting Owl* is a worthy addition to the list. Books about owls ought to reveal an author's feelings about them: This one does just that, but it also gives us a comprehensive review of many aspects of owl biology, a good introduction to owl folklore, and a balanced outlook on conservation issues. I hope that a great many people on both sides of the Atlantic will read it: I have no doubt that all those who do will both enjoy it and learn a great deal from it.

— Mike Everett
The Royal Society for the Protection of Birds

Great horned owl. (Photo © by Lynn Stone)

AN OWL ENCOUNTER

Hooter arrived on a sultry August afternoon in 1980. When we first met, Hooter was an unnamed ball of fluffy brown feathers, a recently fledged great horned owl (*Bubo virginianus*) raised at Audubon Zoo in New Orleans. The orphaned owl, which was nearly seven months old, had been living in a large outdoor cage where it learned to pounce on and eat live mice. Now Anne Tappan, the zoo's raptor rehabilitator, hoped to find a safe place to release the young bird.

At that time we lived on Horn Island, a barrier island ten miles off the Gulf Coast of Mississippi, where my husband Pat worked as a National Park Service ranger. The wilderness island offered acres of slash pine forest seldom trod by human visitors. Chances were good the owl could survive here on its own. So it was that Anne met us on the island after an hour-long boat ride across Mississippi Sound. She had a wide-eyed owlet in tow.

With her gloved hand, Anne gently removed the large bird from its travel cage. The owl blinked at the intense sunlight reflecting from the white sand and stared at its new surroundings.

Anne held the bird firmly while Pat placed a numbered aluminum band on its left leg. Displaying the ferocity that has earned great horned owls the nickname "flying tigers," the owlet gaped, hissed, and clenched its formidable talons into tight fists. Once the band was in place, Anne released the bird, which flew immediately to a nearby pine bough. Though still obviously young and inexperienced, it celebrated freedom with what was meant to be an intimidating display of beak clacking and harsh chattering.

"Keep an eye on it for a few days, if you can," Anne instructed on her way back to the boat. "If it gets really hungry and doesn't seem to be eating, you can toss it a mouse. But it's best to ignore the owl," she reminded, "so it will feed on its own."

Shortly before dusk the following day we heard the clacking of the owl's beak and chittering sounds coming from a cluster of trees east of the ranger station. We approached quietly, but when we were still a hundred feet distant, the bird flew. "Good," we convinced ourselves. "The owl is acclimatizing."

Our sense of well-being was short-lived, however, as the owl reappeared the following day. It perched first on the water tank, then moved to the shed roof, and finally landed on the fence a few feet from our porch door. All the while it hooted and bobbed impatiently as though waiting to be fed. Several resident fish crows and the pair of gray kingbirds that nested next to our porch were aroused by all the ruckus. They chided and dove at the owlet, which was quickly transformed from a bold beggar to a bundle of timidity huddled close to the trunk of a pine tree.

Another day passed, and by this time our guest was howling mad and obviously hungry. It called to us from the porch railing, a window sill, and the doorstep. As I walked out of the house, it swooped low over my head. Fearing that the owl wasn't finding food in this unfamiliar habitat, we offered it a hastily defrosted mouse, which it gulped greedily.

Three more days passed, each with the owl making at least one appearance begging for food. Difficult as it was, we ignored it, following Anne's advice to let it get really hungry. The owl made a final plea about dusk on August 15. Then it disappeared. We did not see or hear the young bird again. Pat failed to locate the carcass on extensive patrols of the island, but we assumed that the owl did not adjust to life here.

Hoo, hoo-hoo-oo, hoo, hoo. Nine weeks later, about two o'clock in the morning, we awakened to a loud thump against the glass of our bedroom window. In the light of a nearly full moon we saw the silhouette of a great horned owl perched on the air conditioner. The bird was peering at us and booming out the deep, resonant song as if (in our anthropomorphic opinion) it had just discovered a long-lost friend. After serenading us from its window perch, the owl flew to the roof, then landed atop the shed, and finally moved to a tree north of the ranger cabin. Each new landing brought a renewed series of enthusiastic hoots. We were overjoyed that somehow the young owl survived and had returned to visit. From then on, we referred to it as "Hooter."

Hooter took up residence near the ranger station. The bird no longer begged to be fed, although when we saw it strutting around the yard like a rooster, pouncing on large insects and lizards, we wondered if it had mastered the art of hunting. Soon after its return, Hooter realized that the maintenance barn harbored plenty of rats and mice. From then on we often noticed the owl sitting watchfully among the rafters.

On many evenings the bird hooted an arrival announcement, then sat at our doorstep. Pat became quite good at imitating the owl's calls, and as winter approached, they had numerous long "conversations."

Hooter's favorite perch was the window air conditioner, where it could watch us as we went about our evening chores. The owl might appear any time from dusk to dawn, but usually it arrived between eight and eleven at night. At first it was a bit unnerving to see a pair of curious yellow eyes staring into our bedroom. But it is a rare treat for rangers on wilderness islands to have friends drop in unexpectedly, so we began to look forward to Hooter's visits. I'm convinced that had we raised the window, Hooter would have hopped into the house. Several times when the bird landed on the doorstep and we opened the door, it peeked in curiously.

Hooter seemed to enjoy company. A group of scientists set up a temporary tent camp near the ranger station late that autumn. The first night, Hooter landed on the tent poles and welcomed them with a lusty serenade. Later in the week as the group ate supper on outdoor picnic tables, the owl watched and offered an echoing song from the shed roof.

Our electricity at the station came from a generator located in a small buildling a hundred yards north of the house. At bedtime, Pat walked up the sandy path to shut the power off for the night. Hooter keyed in on this evening routine and usually greeted Pat with a soft chirring call when he emerged from the now-quiet engine room. Pat "conversed" with the owl as he walked home. Hooter would swoop low over Pat and land ahead of him on the fence near the cabin. If Pat held his arm out to the side, Hooter sometimes hovered above or landed gently, careful not to jab its sharp talons into Pat's sleeve or skin.

I refer to Hooter as "it" because we were never certain of its sex. We have reason to believe, however, that Hooter was a male owl. In late November Hooter arrived at our window with a decapitated mouse in its beak. By this time the owl had become an accomplished predator. Gone were the disheveled feathers of its youth. They were replaced by the sleek, camouflaged plumage of a forest hunter.

Hooter flew to the doorstep and called persistently. The bird's white bib swelled with each hoot, giving Hooter an air of formality akin to a

Once set free, the orphaned owl scolded us with a bold display of chattering and beak clacking. (Photo © by Connie Toops)

dinner guest arriving in white-tie and tails. Pat opened the door and answered, which sent Hooter into an excitedly rising series of *whoo-hoo*s. The owl fluffed up, shuffled its feet, bowed, and eventually offered the mouse to Pat.

Three nights later Hooter appeared at the window with a rabbit's head. It was the same routine. Hooter and Pat exchanged calls, Hooter bowed and shuffled, took the prey from its beak with its talons, and laid it at Pat's feet. This time when Pat reached for the still-warm head, Hooter ruffled and scolded in a high-pitched chirp. The perturbed owl grabbed the offering and flew to a nearby pine. Later, it brought a decapitated rat to the doorstep and again performed the shuffling display.

The owl's visits became quite regular during the next few weeks. Frequently it brought mice. It also offered Pat a dead chickadee and an unidentified robin-sized bird. On evenings when it did not attempt to win our favor with food, Hooter sat on the fence or porch railing and *hoo-hoo*ed with gusto. We suspected that the increased attention Hooter paid to us was related to the fact that great horned owls breed and begin to nest on the Gulf Coast in December.

Sometime later, Canadian owl behavior expert Kay McKeever explained that Hooter heard the calls of its parents while inside its egg, before it hatched, so it communicated through typical owl sounds. But Hooter had visually imprinted on, or identified with, humans. This often happens when well-meaning but untrained people raise wild birds. Instinct directs young owls to imitate and follow their parents from the time their eyes begin to focus until they cease being fed regularly. Unfortunately, Hooter had identified with its rescuers instead of its own species. Although the bird was physically fine, it was psychologically impaired. It would never have the urge to mate with another great horned owl.

Rehabilitators at Audubon Zoo told us that baby great horned owls normally remain with their parents from five to seven months. They beg for food until the adults finally ignore them. Then young birds disperse, but they usually return to the area where they were born to nest. Hooter probably explored the twelve-mile-long island during its two-month absence. Since it did not find its natural birth site, Hooter's instincts guided it back to the release area.

We were away from Horn Island during January and February. When we returned, another ranger filled us in on Hooter's adventures. One night, while a research group camped near the station, Hooter landed on the head of one of the workers. The woman was startled, but unhurt. Several weeks later Hooter buzzed a young camper. For the rest of their visit, the child and his parents were reluctant to set foot outside their tent at night. They happened to mention the incident to the ranger, who explained the owl's history and reassured them somewhat.

As hard as it was for us, we began to ignore Hooter's advances. We thought that by scaring the bird away when it approached humans too closely, we could avoid its developing a "killer owl" image. Hooter's visits did become less frequent during the spring and summer, but the big bird still peered in the bedroom window now and then or called to us as we returned from shutting down the generator.

Our assignment on Horn Island ended a year after Hooter arrived. We later learned that during the next mating season Hooter returned to the station and introduced itself to the new ranger. Kay McKeever's studies show that wild owls think "wild" forever, even if they are caged because of injuries. Conversely, abnormally imprinted owls never learn to be wild. Rehabilitators understand that now and do not release human-imprinted owls. A decade ago when Hooter was released, imprinting was not as clearly understood.

Hooter's overfriendly advances to unsuspecting park visitors continued. Eventually rangers captured and relocated the owl to a privately owned island where there was less chance of human encounters. Because it was imprinted, Hooter never had the opportunity to live as "normal" owls do. Our experience with the bird confirmed my personal conviction—as well as the mandate of federal law—that impaired birds should be raised only by licensed rehabilitators.

Hooter often sat on our porch railing and entertained us with lusty serenades. (Photo © by Connie Toops)

Hooter returned from a nine-week absence an accomplished hunter. The disheveled feathers of its youth were replaced by the sleek, camouflaged plumage of a forest hunter. (Photo © by Connie Toops)

I had, of course, seen and heard other owls before meeting Hooter. Getting to know that owl, though, was a rare privilege. It forever changed my feelings about these magnificent birds of prey. As wardens on a wilderness barrier island, Pat and I were guests in a place where nature took its course regardless of human interference. In a sense, Hooter shared that guest status.

As my fondness for Hooter grew, I unconsciously watched for its shadow moving silently across the ground on moonlit evenings. Many days it sat in a pine tree outside our window, first scrutinizing the nuthatches on the branch above, then staring at us, then observing the nuthatches again.

Sometimes we awoke to see Hooter watching us through the window. As the dawn progressed, Hooter would grow sleepy. Its eyelids drooped to narrow slits. It shifted feet and yawned, throwing its head so far back that the bright pink lining of its mouth showed in sharp

contrast to the mottled brown feathers of its head and neck. If a breeze blew the branch, the owl's body moved. Yet its head and eyes remained motionless, staring curiously at us. Finally it dozed.

Hooter's short naps were interrupted by the snap of a limb or by the mockingbirds and kestrels that mobbed it from nearby branches. The owl roused sluggishly, rubbed its sleepy eyes on its wing, then nuzzled its head onto its breast once more. Day by day we learned more about the owl's behavior and developed a kinship with it. Through Hooter, we bridged a gap that usually separates humans from wildlife. Hooter put us in close touch with the natural world.

Since meeting Hooter, I have developed a deep enchantment with owls in general and great horned owls in particular. I cannot hear the *hoo, hoo-hoo-oo, hoo, hoo* in the night or look into the spirited yellow eyes of one of these beautiful creatures without remembering the bond of trust and friendship we shared with Hooter years ago on a distant island.

Sometimes we awoke to see Hooter peering through our window. (Photo © by Connie Toops)

THE LEGENDARY OWL

For owls, perhaps more than for other members of the animal kingdom, we humans exhibit a special fascination. What is it about a chance encounter with an owl that brings us such delight and at the same time tugs at some primitive sense of awe?

Part of the answer lies in what we see—a creature with an upright stance, round face, high forehead, short "nose," and large, blinking eyes that seem at times capable of human expression. If we allow ourselves to anthropomorphize, we see proportions similar to those of the human face, and sometimes we attribute human qualities to these birds. Owls frequently tolerate our close approach. When we have an opportunity to exchange glances with an owl, there is a fleeting moment of engagement. We recognize each other as living beings. For some observers, trading gazes with an owl symbolizes the beauty and harmony of the natural world.

Others are fascinated by the behavioral parallels between humans and owls. Most owls are monogamous. Many remain true to one mate until death. The owl's life is highly ordered, revolving around a distinct home territory. In a great number of species, the female attends to duties at the nest while the male fills the role of the provider. Humans identify with similar social roles.

Owls have always exerted a strong appeal. Images of owls more than thirty centuries old appear on Chinese bronze containers, Egyptian tombs, and American Indian stone amulets. Owl decoys, as well as coins, stamps, and art objects bearing owl likenesses are in high demand by collectors. Owl motifs decorate everything from corporate advertising to jewelry to doormats. Among birders, elusive species of owls including the great gray owl (*Strix nebulosa*) and hawk owl (*Surnia ulula*) are on "most wanted" lists. Dedicated bird watchers will travel hundreds of miles to catch a glimpse of a snowy owl (*Nyctea scandiaca*) or boreal owl (*Aegolius funereus*) during southern peregrinations of these normally arctic birds. The sight of an owl is so impressive that nonbirders often recall in great detail the bird's appearance and the circumstances under which they viewed it.

Of the 133 species of owls worldwide, about eighty hunt at night. Most of the rest are crepuscular, especially active at dusk and dawn. Through the ages, humans, who possess relatively poor night vision, have been fascinated by the owl's ability to hunt quietly and capture prey in the dark. Ancient people attributed the owl's hunting prowess to its magical powers. Many cultures shared the belief that since owl eyes resemble our own, owls were once human and are now transformed spirits. Various names used to describe owls find roots in these beliefs.

Ancient Greeks observed the little owl (*Athene noctua*) around their orchards, in hedgerows between cultivated fields, even nesting in holes in stone walls and buildings. This small, brown relative of the North American burrowing owl (*Athene cunicularia*) is most active at daybreak and after sunset. It frequently perches on a post or low branch in open view during the day. Its

Ancient Greeks associated little owls with Athena, the goddess of wisdom. (Photo © by Robert Maier, Animals Animals)

15

glowering yellow eyes, combined with pale eyebrow markings and rounded head, give the bird a somber countenance. The first recorded Greek name for this owl is *glaux*, descriptive of the yellow-green sheen of mineral ore and the color of the owl's shining eyes. According to Greek beliefs, these glowing eyes were the magic that allowed the little owl to see at night.

Little owls nested in the Acropolis, the temple of Athena, goddess of wisdom. As generation after generation of Greeks saw these kestrel-sized birds staring out from niches atop the stone pillars of this magnificent building, they began to associate the owls with the wisdom the temple stood for. Owls were not, however, the only birds linked with human powers. Eagles, symbolic of supreme rule, stood for Zeus, the king of Greek gods. Falcon images represented Apollo, the god of light and prophecy, and Aphrodite, goddess of love, was depicted by the dove.

Greeks believed that their goddess of wisdom could transform herself into the form of an owl. In this disguise Athena would roam the countryside to check on her subjects. When a little owl appeared during a battle between Greeks and Persians at Marathon in 490 B.C., the badly outnumbered Greek soldiers thought their goddess had arrived to save them. Athena's presence, symbolized by the owl, promised victory. Her subjects rallied and drove the invading Persians back to their ships. Later, enterprising Greek generals were rumored to carry caged owls among their personal luggage and secretly release them to inspire troops to crucial victories.

So closely were Athena and the little owl associated that after the battle of Marathon a silver tetradrachma coin (roughly equivalent to $20 U.S.) carried the likeness of the goddess on one side and the little owl on the other. At a time when Middle East traders were sometimes suspicious of coinage from other lands, the Greek tetradrachma was always honored for its full worth.

Romans eventually overcame the Greek empire. They, too, adopted the little owl as a symbol of wisdom, but the Romans attributed it to their own goddess, Minerva. As Roman culture spread throughout western Europe, the little owl became known as "Minerva's owl." To this day the Greek goddess Athena and her owl are joined by scientific nomenclature. The genus that contains little and burrowing owls is *Athene*.

Despite the classical associations of owls with wisdom goddesses, it is hard to say whether owls are indeed "wise." Avian and human intelligences are difficult to equate. In Europe barn (*Tyto alba*), long-eared (*Asio otus*), and tawny (*Strix aluco*) owls have been observed flying low over hedgerows, beating their wings on the shrubs to scare out roosting songbirds. Perhaps the owls first flushed such prey by accident, then learned to use the technique for successful hunts. In scientific tests, barn owls learn and remember the differences in sounds made by various prey animals such as mice, shrews, and rats. Tawny owls can remember for up to thirty minutes where a mouse is hidden from view under a box. Neither cats nor raccoons given the same test had that long a recall period, although the owls may have shown such lengthy interest because they heard the mouse inside the box. Tawny owls, called "parliaments" when gathered in small groups, have traditionally been regarded in England as "wise" birds. Yet in Italy, another tradition asserts that the tawny owl is stupid, and it is sometimes portrayed wearing a dunce cap.

Owls' remarkable night hunting skills, however, are probably based less on wisdom than on exceptionally well-developed senses of hearing and sight. Much of an owl's behavior stems from instinctive reaction rather than reasoned thought.

In numerous cultures the owl's reputation for good or evil powers came from its appearance, its sounds, or the places it lived. Since owls inhabit desolate areas and have vocalizations that range from haunting hoots and hollers to spooky shrieks, they evoked fears of death. So strong was this fear among Hindus that if an owl landed on the roof of a hut, the thatch was removed and burned at once. In rural China, the multisyllable

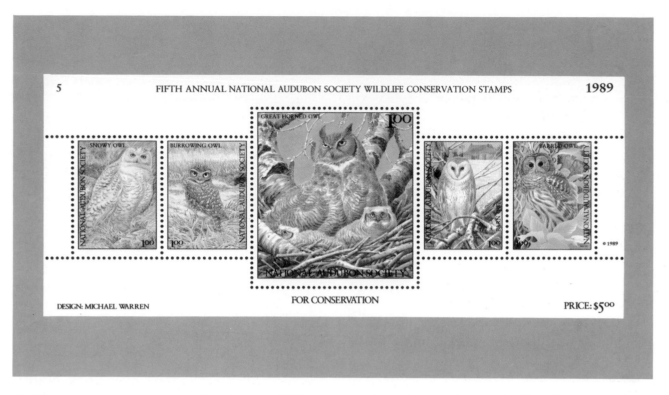

Owl images exert a strong appeal. They decorate wildlife stamps, jewelry, and a host of other collectibles. (Courtesy National Audubon Society and Unicover Corp.)

Owls are widely reproduced in art. This great horned owl was painted by Navajo artist Beatien Yazz. (Photo of "Owl on a Limb with Yellow Moon Shining," in the collection of Stuart Maule, by Jeff Glickman)

Owl likenesses appear on postage stamps from several nations. (Photo © by Connie Toops)

Owls have always been victims of ignorance and superstition, believed to be birds of ill omen and harbingers of misfortune and death.—Arthur Cleveland Bent, Life Histories of North American Birds of Prey *(Photo © by Connie Toops)*

hoot of an owl is interpreted as "Go dig your grave."

Pliny, a first-century Roman scholar, wrote in his *Natural History* of the "scritch-owl" as a "monster of the night, neither crying nor singing out clear, but uttering a certain groan of doleful meaning." Elsewhere Pliny referred to owls as "the funeral birds of the night." So great was the fear of "death owls" that Romans killed them when heard. In order to prevent fulfillment of death prophecies, Romans cremated owl corpses and threw the ashes into the Tiber River. When the Swedish taxonomist Linnaeus named the boreal owl in 1758, he chose the scientific name *funereus*, or "funereal owl."

The association of owls with death continued through feudal times when a family member was believed to be doomed if an owl perched on a castle. Edmund Spenser, a sixteenth-century English poet, characterized the owl as "death's dread messenger."

Since eerie nighttime hoots aroused human fears of darkness, owls began to be linked with witches. In both Greek and Latin the word *strix* means "owl." It is akin to the Latin *stridens*, describing harsh, witchlike, discordant sounds. Anglo-Saxon tales refer to both owls and witches as "hags." American Indians of the Cherokee tribe used *tskili* with a similar dual meaning.

French names for owls, however, show that the birds were held in high esteem. *Hibou grand-duc* describes the majestic eagle owl (*Bubo bubo*), France's largest owl. The title, which suggests the owl has the noble rank of a grand duke, is based on the hierarchy of French monarchs. Centuries ago a noble who ranked less than a duke could not wear erect feather plumes as part of his headgear. Therefore, the French tufted owls were believed to be royalty. In addition to

It was the owl that shrieked, the fatal bellman which gives the stern'st goodnight.—William Shakespeare, Macbeth *(Photo © by Breck Kent)*

Owl-related words are taken from the sound of the owls' voices. The Roman name for eagle owl, bubo, imitated its descending hoots, oohu . . . oohu . . . oohu. (Photo © by Henry Ausloos, Animals Animals)

the eagle owl, the medium-sized long-eared owl and the smaller scops owl (*Otus scops*) bore the royal names *hibou moyen-duc* (middle duke) and *hibou petit-duc* (little duke).

Elsewhere, owl-related words developed from the birds' voices. The ancient Roman name for the eagle owl, *bubo*, imitated its descending *oo-hu. . . oohu. . . oohu.* Modern local European names are also interpretations of this sound. Eagle owls are called *uhu* in Germany, *buhu* in Spain, *gufo* in Italy, and *oehoe* in Holland.

Wild eagle owls no longer visit the British Isles but the familiar *tu-whit-tu-whoo* of the tawny owl rings out during the night throughout England, Scotland, and Wales. Barn owls are seen regularly at dusk, hunting along roadsides and over grassy fields. According to folklorist Virginia Holmgren, the Old English interpretations of owl hoots—*howyelle, hoole, oule,* and *owell*—later came to mean "owl," the bird, and "howl" and "yowl," its sounds. The strident voice of the barn owl, a lesser-known but eerie night sound associated with church belfries and barnyards, is also mentioned in British literature. Interestingly, when Shakespeare and other writers of his era referred to a "screech owl," they meant the owl we know today as the barn owl. English settlers in the New World, however, applied the title "screech owl" to the smaller North American species, *Otus asio*, the eastern screech owl that calls with a whinnying trill.

Although the barn owl was labeled as a "death owl" throughout Britain, it is called *barbagianni* (from *barba*, beard) and *zio* (uncle) in villages of rural Italy. Both titles indicate the respect shown for the owl, which is held in the same esteem as white-bearded senior members of the community. Genghis Khan, a twelfth-century Mongolian warrior, attributed a barn owl with saving his life by showing him a safe refuge from his enemies one night. Thereafter Khan and his followers wore owl feathers in their hats and carried owl amulets for good luck.

Similarly, owls were highly regarded in the folklore of numerous other cultures. North American Creek Indians, who lived in southeastern parts of the United States, considered great horned owls a symbol of divine wisdom. Each Creek medicine man wore a realistically stuffed owl in his headdress or attached as if perched on his arm. The owl, known as a "magic-maker," was believed to be in contact with the spirit world. Only the spiritual leader of the tribe could ask advice of the bird. Anyone unlucky enough to be crossed by the shadow of a live flying owl was thought to be cursed and could expect to become ill in punishment for his or her evil deeds.

Owls figure prominently in creation stories of the Cherokee, Menominee, and Apache Indians. People of the Pueblo tribe are especially keen observers of nature. Their legends distinguish among seven species of owls. Zuni Indians believe each of their native owl species has a particular gift or task. The burrowing owl is for them a special benefactor, known as the "priest of prairie dogs." Hopis trust in this owl, which nests underground, as the keeper of the dead. It also has the power to keep fires burning and to germinate seeds.

Pima Indians of the American Southwest believe that at death, one's soul passes into the body of a screech or great horned owl. According to J. R. Swanton, a government ethnologist who studied a group of Pimas in Arizona in 1904:

Should an owl happen to be hooting at the time of a death, it was believed that it was waiting for the soul. . . . Owl feathers were always given to a dying person. They were kept in a long, rectangular box or basket of maguey leaf. If the family had no owl feathers at hand, they sent to the medicine-man who always kept them. If possible, the feathers were taken from a living bird.

Shamans frequently raised young owls. Pimas placed owl feathers in the hands of tribe members about to die, or on their doorstep or on a path they had frequently walked. Prayer dancers imitated the clicking call of the screech owl with pebbles shaken in a hollow gourd. Supposedly the owl would see the feathers and know that the soul of the dying person was ready for its journey. Pimas believed that a few of their tribal members were honored by becoming owls in the

There came a gray owl at sunset,
  There came a gray owl at sunset,
Hooting softly around me,
  He brought terror to my heart.
—*Translated from a Pima Indian song.*
(Photo © by Jeff Foott)

The grave owl with wisdom fraught
  In sober, solemn silence sits.
—*Anonymous (1791) (Photo © by Jeff Foott)*

afterlife and they returned to departed kin to ease the journey to death.

Another belief shared by cultures around the world was the medical theory that if you had a troubled body part, you should treat it with a similar part from a plant or an animal. Because of owls' spiritual powers, they were in high demand in many folk remedies and great numbers of these birds must have been killed through the centuries.

Owl eyes were a popular ingredient for such concoctions. Europeans charred, then dried and ground owl eyes into a powder used to remedy failing eyesight and insanity. In India, a brew of owl eyes was thought to cure children with seizures. Ancient Romans, as well as Moroccans centuries later, believed that a preserved owl eye worn as a necklace warded off evil. In central Europe, a soldier carrying an owl's heart into battle would be brave, while in Old England an owl's foot or the whole bird stuffed and attached to a cradle summoned good health to a young child.

European superstition dictated that a woman would not have a son if while pregnant she heard an owl hoot. In India, drinking a potion that con-

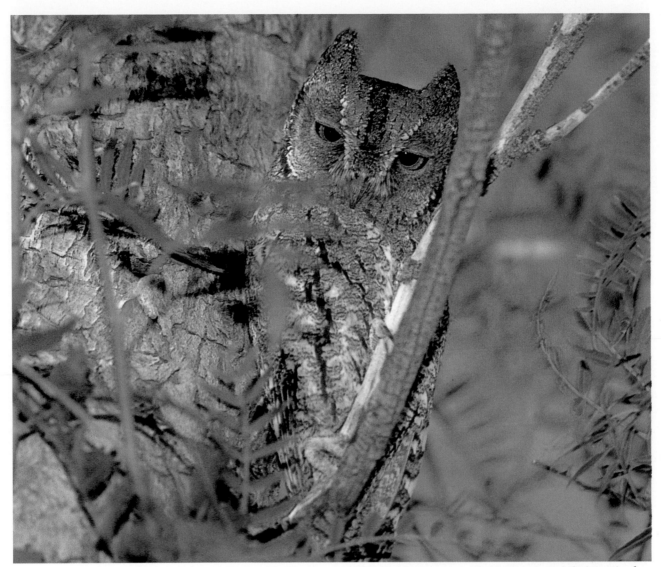

The scops owl, the smallest of the tufted owls native to France, was thought to be royalty. The French name hibou petit-duc *means "little duke." (Photo © by Arthur Gloor, Animals Animals)*

tained owl brain before she went into labor supposedly insured the mother of a healthy baby. Feeding a child owl broth continued its good fortune in life. In England owl stew was thought to prevent whooping cough in children and ward off drunkenness in later life. An alcoholic could be cured by eating owl eggs raw or pickled in wine for three days. Owl liver or brains mixed in olive oil were used to treat earaches. Owl brains could also be boiled in sea water until they gelled, then applied as a suppository to end constipation. Until fairly recently, nailing a dead owl or its wings to a European home or barn was believed to ward off plagues and storms.

The Micmac Indians of New Brunswick, on the other hand, venerated live owls. According to one of their legends, the Golden Age was a mythical time when people and animals lived in perfect harmony. The age ended when the animals began to quarrel and this disgusted the Micmac god, Glooscap. He left, saying he would not return until the differences were settled. The owl was so saddened that it cried, *Koo-kooshoos,* meaning "I am sorry." Even today, several Indian tribes believe that the hoot of the owl is a cry of sadness for the lost harmony of the world.

OWL ORIGINS AND DISTRIBUTION

The record of ancient bird remains is sketchy. Fragile bird bones were less frequently fossilized than the heavier skeletons of mammals and reptiles. The earliest fossils attributed to a birdlike creature are those of *Archaeopteryx*, discovered in 1861 in a West German limestone quarry.

Archaeopteryx lived 140 million years ago, at a time when the landmasses we now know as separate continents were still joined. Dinosaurs were the dominant animals, enjoying worldwide temperatures much warmer than they are at present.

The scaled head of *Archaeopteryx* resembled that of a lizard. Like small dinosaurs, its jaws were lined with sharp teeth and its digits tipped with claws. But this crow-sized creature had one important characteristic—feathers—that separated it from the reptiles. Scientists do not know whether *Archaeopteryx* jumped and glided from one branch to the next or whether it had mastered free flight. Its feathers, however, look much like those of modern birds.

About 120 million years ago the landmass that became North and South America began to break free of what became Africa and Southern Europe, forming an ever-widening rift that was filled by the Atlantic Ocean. The few bird fossils known from this period come from the American Midwest and central Mongolia. Fossils from Kansas are of water birds, not surprising since the area was inundated at that time by a shallow sea. One Kansan fossil resembles a loon and another a tern, though neither are direct ancestors of these species. Modern avian families began to

evolve about 65 to 70 million years ago. At that time, tropical and subtropical plants extended north to what is now France, southern England, and southern Canada. Temperate trees, including willow, pine, spruce, and birch flourished into the far north.

The continents continued drifting apart, although the seas separating northern Europe, Greenland, and northern North America were not as wide as they are today. Alaska and Siberia were still joined by a land bridge, thus plant and animal communities of Eurasia and North America were similar.

Some 100 million years ago owls and nightjars may have shared common ancestors. Nightjars include night-feeding oilbirds, whip-poor-wills, and nighthawks. Most of the birds in this order live in temperate or tropical habitats and eat insects. They have mottled plumage in earthy colors that camouflages them on their daytime roosts. Although owl feather patterns are much the same as nightjars', owls evolved separately, specializing as rodent-eaters.

Owl beaks and talons resemble those of hawks, a likeness believed to be the result of convergent evolution. This theory explains similarities in unrelated hawks and owls by citing their development to fill analogous ecological niches. That is, since hawks and owls eat similar prey, curved beaks and hooked talons with gripping pads on the bottoms of the feet are valuable to both groups.

The oldest owl fossils from North America are

The elf owl, measuring only five inches tall, is the smallest of nineteen owl species that live north of the United States–Mexican border. (Photo © by Allan Morgan)

Owls appeared about 60 million years ago. At that time the earth was warmer than it is now, and subtropical plants flourished as far north as France, England, and Canada. (Photo © by Connie Toops)

Plants and animals of temperate deciduous forests retreated south ahead of advancing ice during glacial periods. (Photo © by Maslowski Wildlife Productions)

Snowy owls nest on the northern fringes of the North American and Eurasian continents. In winters when their primary food sources — lemmings and hares — are scarce, snowy owls wander far to the south in search of prey. (Photo © by Richard Smith)

about 60 million years old and are an intermediate form between barn owls (Tytonidae) and typical owls (Strigidae). Other prehistoric owls that inhabited the American West are known from fossil records dating to 50 million years ago. Remains ranging from 27 to 45 million years of age indicate that ancestors of the eagle, long-eared, and short-eared owls lived in France at that time. Two legbone fossils found in Romania suggest predecessors of modern owls lived there at least 10 million years ago. Scientists postulate that more species of owls inhabited Europe 30 million years ago than now.

Around 5 million years ago, temperatures cooled to the point that oaks and other deciduous trees in northern forests were replaced by spruces, firs, and larches. Climatologists theorize that Asian heartlands experienced colder temperatures than those in North America. Using the Bering land bridge, Eurasian species dispersed much more widely into North America, which would have had a milder climate, than North

American species colonized Eurasia. Scientists believe North American species were hampered by their lack of cold-hardiness. They speculate that ancestors of modern owls developed in Eurasia and reached North America via Siberia and Alaska. Many mammals — such as wolves, lynx, hares, marmots, and martins — share this Holarctic distribution.

The Pleistocene Epoch, or Ice Age, included four periods in which glaciers radiated from centers in Scandinavia, the European Alps, Greenland, and Canada. During these glacial cold spells, which lasted up to 50,000 years, plants and animals retreated south ahead of the advancing ice. Fossils of the great gray owl, for instance, were discovered in Romania, at least six hundred miles south of the current limit of this owl's range. Warming spells between glacial periods allowed temperate species to disperse northward once more.

Although owls and hawks are not closely related, they eat similar prey. Thus, they have similar beaks and talons. Barred owls and red-shouldered hawks occupy the same habitats, with the hawks hunting by day and the owls feeding primarily at night. (Photo © by Ronald Morreim)

Short-eared owls inhabit cool regions of North America, South America, Europe, and Asia as well as the Galapagos and Hawaiian islands. (Photo © by Maslowski Wildlife Productions)

Presently owls live on all continents except Antarctica. One of the most cosmopolitan species is the barn owl, which inhabits temperate and tropical regions of North and South America, western Europe, Africa, the Middle East, India, Southeast Asia, and Australia. The short-eared owl (*Asio flammeus*) is also distributed worldwide. Its breeding range includes temperate and boreal regions of North America above 40 degrees north latitude and in Eurasia, similar areas northward from about 45 degrees north latitude. In winter these owls migrate south to Mexico, central Africa, southern India, and southeast Asia. Short-eared owls also reside in cooler regions of South America and are established on oceanic islands including Hawaii, the Galápagos, and the Carolines.

Thirteen species of owls nest in Europe. The greatest variety of species, ten, occurs at about 57 degrees north latitude, along an imaginary line that bisects Scotland, Denmark, southern Sweden, and Latvia. In the Northern Hemisphere, the highest number of owl species is found in Panama. A high incidence of similar species suggests that prey is abundant. In such situations, competitors specialize to make use of as many prey types and ecological niches as possible. In areas home to a number of owl species, some owls inhabit forests while others frequent marshes and meadows. Some eat rodents; others concentrate on catching insects. In these areas, there are both daytime and nighttime hunters.

Nineteen species of owls live north of the United States-Mexican border. Owls that inhabit arid areas of the American Southwest are generally small insect-eaters. Those of boreal forest and arctic habitats are larger and prey on mammals or other birds. The elf owl (*Microathene whitneyi*), at five inches tall, is the smallest North American owl. It nests in abandoned woodpecker holes in saguaro cacti and in hardwood trees along river corridors. Elf owls venture out at night to catch beetles, crickets, spiders, and scorpions. Their fluttering, hovering flight resembles that of a giant moth.

More species of owls (thirteen) can be found in southern Arizona during the spring and summer than in any other region of the United States or

Ancestors of modern owls evolved in Eurasia and dispersed into North America across the Bering land bridge. The great gray is one of seven species of owls that inhabit both the Old and New worlds. (Photo © by Thomas Mangelson)

Canada. In addition to the tiny elf owl, the insectivorous flammulated owl (*Otus flammeolus*) migrates north from Mexico into western ponderosa pine and Douglas fir forests each summer. Two other primarily Central American species, the ferruginous pygmy owl (*Glaucidium brasilianum*) and the whiskered screech owl (*Otus trichopsis*) reach their northern limits in the southeastern corner of Arizona.

The great horned owl is a master of living in varied habitats. It is the most widespread species in North America. Great horned owls reside in every Canadian province and all states except Hawaii. They survive by eating a wide range of prey, from mice to skunks to squirrels.

Europe and North America share seven species of owls. These are the barn, snowy, northern hawk, great gray, long-eared, short-eared, and boreal owls. (In Europe the boreal owl is better known as Tengmalm's owl.) Additional European and North American owls resemble each other physically and share similar habitat requirements. Visitors to the United States may mistake the forest-dwelling barred owl (*Strix varia*) for the tawny owl, a common resident throughout England, Scotland, continental Europe, and portions of Russia, central Asia, and China. Both species have dark eyes and rounded faces with somber expressions.

Early explorers in North America assumed the great horned owl was simply another color variation of the European eagle owl. Plumage of all ten races of eagle owls and twelve races of great horned owls varies from dark markings in wooded areas to pale feathering in desert and taiga surroundings. Not until 1788 was the great horned recognized as a separate species.

Other similar owls are the Old World scops owl and the North American flammulated owl, which prey heavily on insects and invertebrates. The Eurasian pygmy owl (*Glaucidium passerinum*) and its New World relative, the northern pygmy owl (*Glaucidium gnoma*), are shrikelike hunters. Both capture birds and mammals nearly as large as themselves. These European and North American owls that look and behave so much alike undoubtedly descended from common ancestors.

There are twelve subspecies of great horned owls in North America. Their coloration varies from pale feathers in desert and taiga habitats to dark markings in forested areas. This bird, photographed in western Canada, represents the subarctic race. (Photo © by Thomas Mangelson)

AMAZING ADAPTATIONS FOR SEEING & HEARING

Owls, in their various forms, have successfully hunted the earth's forests and meadows for nearly 60 million years. Why have they prospered?

Imagine yourself camping on a moonless night. You hear a rustle in the leaves nearby. If you had to catch this small animal and eat it in order to survive, could you do it? Owls do, routinely. Of great help to owls are amazingly keen night vision and precise hearing. Owls are better than all other birds, under low light conditions, at seeing prey and locating sounds.

Owls have flattened facial discs with large, forward-looking eyes. A human's eyes and those of the largest owl species—eagle, great horned, and snowy—are all about the same size. Yet the average person stands some four feet taller and weighs about fifty times more than these owls do. In comparison to humans, a much larger percentage of the owl's body is devoted to its sense of sight. If human bodies were constructed on owl proportions, our heads would be as large as a washtub to accommodate our upscaled eyes.

An owl's eyes are surrounded by bony tubes in the skull, called scleral ossicles. Owl eyes do not move freely, as do those of humans. Instead, the owl must rotate its entire head by flexing its neck. Looking first over one shoulder, then the other, an owl can turn its head 370 degrees.

Like people, owls have binocular vision. We judge the position of an object in front of us by viewing it with both eyes at the same time. For humans, the total field of vision covers 180 degrees, with the central 140 degrees in binocular view. Owl eyes are not spaced as far apart as our own, and owls do not have as great a field of binocular vision. They see a total of 110 degrees with only 60 to 70 degrees viewed in stereo. To aid both depth perception and their precise method of hearing, owls bob their heads up, down, and sideways, pausing briefly in each new position to stare at an unfamiliar object. The audiovisual clues gained from each minutely different head position give the owls a three-dimensional understanding of the object under scrutiny.

Although owl eyes and human eyes function similarly, owl eyes are superior in their light-gathering and image-resolution abilities. Owl eyes are more elongated than human eyes. Since the cornea and lens are frontmost, a maximum amount of light can enter. This results in a larger image being focused on the light-sensitive retinal cells, called rods and cones, at the back of an owl's eye. The larger image allows owls to see in greater detail.

Consider a camera with an adjustable aperture. To take a picture in dim light, you must open the aperture wide to allow in all the light it is possible for the lens to gather. Owl eyes gather light effectively, with the widest pupil opening for a tawny owl about three times the relative size of human pupil openings.

The folk belief that owls are blinded by daylight is not true. Just as human irises narrow and widen to adjust the amount of light entering the

Barn owls see well in dim light and locate prey accurately by sound. (Photo © by Joe McDonald)

33

Owls are not blinded by daylight. The iris, or colored portion of the eye, constricts during the day to allow only small amounts of light to enter. (Photo © by Ronald Morreim)

eye, so do owls'. During the daytime, owl irises constrict so that only a tiny hole is available for light to penetrate. At night, the iris is drawn back so the pupil is wide open. While human iris muscles come in shades of brown, blue, and green, owl irises are bright yellow in the majority of species. Several varieties, including barn, barred, spotted (*Strix occidentalis*), tawny, Ural (*Strix uralensis*), and flammulated owls, have dark brown irises.

Owls see well at a distance. Great gray owls, for example, can spot mice and voles up to two hundred yards away. Daylight-hunting great gray and Ural owls have smaller eyes than their close relatives, barred and tawny owls, which hunt mainly at night. The muscles in owls' eyes adjust rapidly from near to far vision and vice versa. Tests on northern hawk owls reveal that their eyes focus ten times faster than human eyes do.

Owls focus best on objects at least several feet in front of them and below eye level. Occasional-ly when a bird or some other object of interest is above it, an owl will turn its head upside down to get a better view. Great horned owls cannot clearly see subjects much closer than a yard away. Smaller owls can focus on objects a little nearer, perhaps because they have evolved to catch tiny insects with precision rather than to grab creatures the size of rats, rabbits, and skunks. Most owls close their eyes an instant before they grasp victims, probably to protect these delicate organs. Owls have stiff, whiskerlike bristle feathers surrounding their beaks. They are touch receptors that assist owls in judging prey or hazards close to their faces.

Do owls see in color? The ratio of rods (sensors of shape and movement) to cones (color receptors) in little owls is twelve to one. This means that compared to a human, the little owl would see better in dim light but would have less distinction of color. What people interpret as black in low light appears to owls as various shades of gray. Little owls do recognize yellow, green, and

Owl are better than all other birds at seeing prey in low-light conditions. Many owls see better at night than humans do in daylight. (Photo © by Michael Quinton)

blue in color tests, but red and gray must seem similar to them.

Another way to compare the visual skills of owls and humans is to picture yourself in a meadow on a night when only a few stars are visible. You would barely be able to distinguish objects around you. The same would be true for a pygmy owl, which has the poorest night vision of all owls thus far tested. A tawny owl, however, would be able to see well (though in monochrome shades rather than color) on the same night under the even darker canopy of a deciduous forest. Barn owls possess the amazing ability to negotiate around obstacles within a familiar territory in light thirty-five times less than the starlit meadow.

Owl ears are also quite sensitive and specialized. The feather tufts on "eared" species such as the screech, scops, long-eared, short-eared, great horned, and eagle owls play no role in hearing. Owl ear openings are actually located on the edge of the facial disc, behind the eye. This part of the facial ruff is fringed with short, stiff feathers that gather and amplify sounds. The ear openings are hidden beneath thin, airy feathers that let sounds penetrate freely.

Whereas most birds have small, rounded ear holes, owls have oblong ear openings. Owls are the only birds that possess front and back skin flaps bordering these openings. The flaps are controlled by muscles, used much as deer or rabbits move their external ears. Inner ear development is quite specialized. Owls have the largest avian ear drums and more auditory nerve cells in the brain, comparable to their size, than any other birds.

A difference between the two major groups of owls shows in the shape and position of the ear opening. Members of the barn owl group, which differentiated from typical owls more than 10 million years ago, have unequal ear openings.

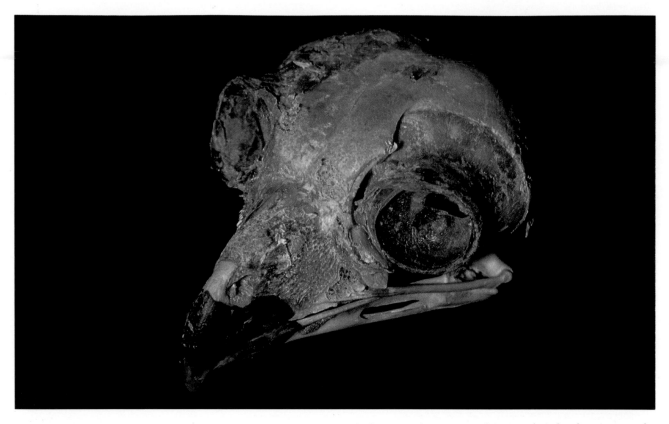

Owl eyes are fixed firmly within bony sockets in the skull. Instead of moving their eyes, owls rotate their heads on extremely lithe necks. (Photo © by Connie Toops)

The left ear and the associated external skin flap are located at a level just above the midpoint of the left eye, while the right ear opening and skin flap are below the midpoint of the right eye.

A number of the strigid (typical) owl group have more pronounced asymmetrical ear openings. These owls have right ears that may be up to 50 percent larger than their left ears. The right ear is also positioned slightly higher than the left. Although in most species these anatomical differences are limited to the fleshy outer structures, great gray, Ural, boreal, and northern saw-whet (*Aegolius acadius*) owl skulls are asymmetrical. The resulting uneven head shape, appearing swollen on the bird's right side, is noticeable in first-hand observations and in photos of front-facing birds.

What connection do these unusual anatomical features have with an owl's ability to catch prey at night? In the 1950s and 1960s scientist Roger Payne studied the hunting prowess of several captive barn owls. He photographed barn owls feeding under normal light conditions. The owls would take off from a perch, flapping and gliding until they reached a point slightly above and behind their prey. An instant before impact, they would swing their feet forward, raise their heads over their shoulders, slow their descent by fully extending their wings, and grab the mouse with outstretched talons.

Using infrared film, Payne photographed barn owls hunting in a totally dark room. He discovered that other than flapping and swinging their legs more in flight, the barn owls captured prey in the dark exactly the same way.

Payne then placed an owl in a dark room that had dry leaves scattered on the floor and released a mouse. The owl pounced on the prey as it rustled through the leaves. Payne repeated the experiment with sand on the floor, to quiet the mouse's footsteps. He tied a wad of noisy crumpled paper to the mouse's tail. The owl unfailingly attacked the paper. To make certain the owl was not detecting infrared body heat or an aroma

Unequally sized ear openings allow owls to locate sounds precisely. The skull of the saw-whet owl appears swollen on the bird's right, the result of having a larger ear opening on that side. (Photo © by Breck Kent)

Owls do not emit sonar. Instead they rely on sounds made by their prey. Their hearing is most acute in the higher frequencies, the range of rodents' shrill squeaks. (Photo © by Maslowski Wildlife Productions)

from the mouse, Payne placed a loudspeaker in the darkened room. As soon as mouse sounds were broadcast, the owl pounced on the speaker. Thus Payne proved barn owls could hunt in total darkness using only their sense of hearing. They are much less effective at catching prey, however, if other sounds, such as wind and rain interfere with auditory reception.

Masakazu Konishi later refined some of Payne's experiments. He found that barn owls associate the noises made by common prey species with these animals. Thus on a dark night, barn owls recognize a shrew noise as a signal for a meal and a skunk noise as something to avoid.

In *Life Histories of North American Birds of Prey*, A. C. Bent recounts the experiences of Charles A. Urner, who was exploring a wetland several decades ago. In the early evening Urner heard shorebirds calling and imitated their sounds. Urner continued:

"Suddenly a Short-eared Owl came out of the growing

darkness and dove at my straw hat. He missed by inches. I whistled the Yellow-legs call again. He turned and dove at me the second time with no end of determination in his manner. Six times I whistled and six times he turned and swooped at me, finally alighting on a mud pile nearby to look the situation over more carefully. I stood in the open marsh with no protection. Had I whistled in the daylight he would have shown no interest. Apparently he did not recognize me as a human in the dusk. He struck on the impulse of his ears — not his eyes. And apparently he knew the taste of Yellowlegs."

Owls do not emit sonar, as bats and dolphins use to find their prey. Owls rely on sounds made by their quarry. Once prey is heard, an owl rapidly turns its head to face the noise. Owls cannot locate a noise accurately with one ear plugged. Konishi discovered that owls pinpoint prey locations to their right or left by timing the interval it takes the sound to reach first one ear, then the other. Konishi has shown that barn owls can discern sound time lags as short as a one hun-

Great horned owl eyes focus best on subjects at least a yard away. Like most owls, they see distant objects quite clearly. (Photo © by Gary Meszaros)

Tawny owls see well on even the darkest nights. To them, a moonless, overcast evening is probably no dimmer than a cloudy day to humans. Tawny owl hearing is ten times more acute than the average person's. (Photo © by D. H. Thompson, Animals Animals)

dred thousandth of a second.

For instance, if a vole (meadow mouse) rustles in the grass to the right of a perched barn owl, the sound will reach the owl's right ear slightly before it reaches the left ear. Almost instantly the owl rotates its head to the right. It stops turning when sounds from the vole equalize in both ears. Thus the owl faces the noise.

How far away is the vole? Sound-catching bristle feathers of the owl's left ruff and earflap tilt down. Those of its right earflap and ruff point upward. Each is like a tiny satellite dish, receiving and focusing sounds into the ear. When noises originate below eye level, they are louder in the left ear. Sounds emanating from above eye level are louder in the right ear. Once the owl has turned its head laterally toward the direction of the sound, it then raises or lowers its face until the volume is equal in both ears. It is now looking directly at its prey, even if there is not enough light to see it.

Strigid owls home in on their victims in much the same way. Instead of upward- and downward-pointing facial ruffs, however, they have unequal ear openings. Nocturnal species— among them the tawny, great gray, long-eared, boreal, and saw-whet owls—have the most highly specialized facial sound collectors. This characteristic is not as pronounced in daylight hunters such as snowy and burrowing owls.

The boreal owl, which has its right ear higher and with a larger sound hole opening than the left, typically sits on low perches and listens for noises made by rodents scampering about on the floor of a coniferous forest. When the owl hears something, it quickly turns toward the noise. Lowering its head and appearing to look hard in that direction, the boreal owl is pinpointing the location by equalizing the sounds. In so doing, it stares directly at the quarry.

To capture the animal, the boreal owl makes a short flight, flapping first to gain speed, then gliding the final yard or so. It fans its wings and tail to brake for the kill. As it slows, it thrusts its feet forward with talons spread. Rodents or other small prey animals are usually paralyzed by the impact of the claws and killed with a quick bite to the neck.

What if the prey makes noise only for a short time? If the animal is located within 30 degrees to the right or left of the center of a barn owl's face, the owl can pinpoint the prey's position without turning its head. Owls have a sizeable region in the sound-recognizing midbrain that is sensitive to time and noise intensity differences. Cells in the front of this brain space are stimulated only by sounds in front of the owl. Brain cells on the right and left sides respond to corresponding sounds to the right or left of the bird. This region of the brain serves as a map to which the owl can assign three-dimensional locations.

All of this takes place amazingly fast. Barn owls can leave their perches within one-half second of hearing prey. In darkness they swoop toward the sound at speeds of up to twelve feet per second. Owls can also make midflight corrections if they hear the prey move while they are en route.

Owls hear the faintest sounds and the widest range of frequencies of all birds thus far studied. Human hearing is most acute at about one kilohertz, the tone of the sixth octave C on a piano. Humans do hear both lower and slightly higher pitches than most owls can. The boreal owl, with its exaggerated asymmetrical ears, hears better than all other owls in the range of twelve to fifteen kilohertz. These high frequencies approach the upper limit of human hearing.

Within the range of four-tenths to eight kilohertz, roughly the A above middle C to the uppermost note on a piano, owls hear sounds better than humans do. At the high end of the scale— sounds equal to shrill rodent squeaks—cats and owls hear similarly. For the pitches equivalent to the top two octaves on a piano, the hearing of tawny and long-eared owls is ten times better than that of humans.

Therefore, if a vole rustles in the grass or a shrew squeaks when an owl is nearby on very dark night, the owl is well-equipped to pinpoint its location.

Boreal owls hunt by perching on a branch and listening intently. They nab unwary prey by making a short, quiet flight and then swooping down at the last moment to stun their quarry with the impact of their claws. (Photo © by Gary Meszaros)

Great Gray Owl Hunting: *A great gray owl listens attentively from a perch at the edge of the forest. Its prey may be a vole scampering through the grass or a pocket gopher tunneling underground. (Photo © by Glenn Van Nimwegen)*

Great Gray Owl Hunting: *Once the owl hears its prey, it slips from its perch and glides toward the unsuspecting rodent. Sometimes the owl hovers momentarily over the animal to make certain of its location. (Photo © by Glenn Van Nimwegen)*

Great Gray Owl Hunting: *The owl dives head-first. If its prey is a pocket gopher in its underground tunnel, the owl thrusts its feet into the snow or loose soil as it lands, stunning the little creature with its talons. It kills the catch with a bite to the back of the neck. (Photo © by Glenn Van Nimwegen)* 44

Great Gray Owl Hunting: *Once prey is captured, the owl flies to a perch, holding dinner securely in its talons. The great gray will then eat the small rodent in one or two gulps. (Photo © by Glenn Van Nimwegen)*

Great Gray Owl Hunting: *Not all hunting forays are successful. Although the owl missed this time, it will return to a listening post and try again. (Photo © by Glenn Van Nimwegen)*

Cryptically colored feathers hide great gray owls from predators and prey. (Photo © by Gary Meszaros)

HUNTING ON HUSHED WINGS

Unnoticed by most passing humans and many creatures of the lodgepole pine forest in Wyoming's Yellowstone Basin, a great gray owl sits quietly in the fading light. The dusky, mottled feathers on the motionless bird—barred on the breast and forming light and dark concentric circles on the facial disc—match the texture and colors of the tree trunk behind it.

The owl sleeps, but now and then some distant sound arouses its curiosity. Inquisitive yellow eyes gaze in that direction for a few moments, then disappear once more under heavy eyelids. Suddenly the owl snaps to attention, its focus fixed on a patch of sparse grasses twenty-five yards away. All around on the forest floor are trails of damp brown earth, pushed up by pocket gophers tunneling under the surface.

The owl cocks its head and stares hypnotically at the ground. As it watches, a bulge of chocolate-colored dirt wells up from below. The owl's wings flick in anticipation. It shifts weight from one foot to the other. Another upwelling of moist, dark soil spews out beneath a grass clump.

Without making a sound, the owl spreads its wings a full five feet and sails into the air. It hovers for a moment with head down, then arches its wings and drops. A hollow thud echoes through the silent forest as the owl's talons sink into the soft earth. With one quick squeeze, the little miner below is pinned amid sharp talons.

The owl tucks its mantling wings back into place and stands upright. It jerks a foot out of the tunnel and for the first time sees its chubby prey. One quick bite behind the skull ends the gopher's life. The owl grasps the rodent in its beak and flies silently to a new perch near another lodgepole trunk. There, camouflaged once more against the dappled bark, it gulps down the gopher.

The Dakota Indian name for owl means "night bird who hunts with hushed wings." In addition to excellent hearing and vision, the thirty-three species of owls native to temperate, boreal, and arctic regions of the Northern Hemisphere share other traits that make them excellent hunters. One of the most useful is the ability to move stealthily from place to place. Equally important is being able to blend with the surroundings when sitting still.

Even the smallest owls are covered with thousands of feathers of several specialized types. Insulating down and fluffy semiplume feathers lie next to an owl's body. These are, for the most part, hidden beneath an outer layer of smooth contour feathers. Owls of northern climates, such as the snowy, have downy feathers that insulate their legs, while burrowing and barn owls, which live in temperate zones, have sparse leg feathering. The great gray owl's size is deceptive. Outwardly it surpasses the height and wing length of the snowy owl, but great grays weigh

a third less. Much of their apparent bulk consists of airy contour and semiplume feathers.

If you look closely at a contour feather from any bird, you will see diagonal branches, called barbs, attached to the central shaft. Hundreds of tiny Velcrolike hooks diverge from each barb. These barbules lock together so the feather will shed water and support the bird in flight. Barbs may separate as the birds feed or fly, so owls spend hours every day running their beaks from the base to the tip of each contour feather, cleaning and straightening them. If you have ever pulled a feather through your fingers and watched the separated edges close like a zipper, you have imitated a preening bird.

Owl feathers are very supple and have soft, fringelike edges that muffle sounds. The flight feathers on an owl's wing are especially interesting. Owls differ from other birds in that the barbules of feathers on the leading edge of their wings do not interlock. Instead, the margins of the outermost flight feathers are separated, like teeth in a comb. These feathers slice through air currents silently instead of thumping into the air as the more "solid" edges of feathers on other birds wings do.

Owl wings are broad, rounded, and large in proportion to the bird's body weight. In aerodynamic terms, most owls have a low wing-loading value. This means they glide buoyantly and fly with a minimum of effort, flapping, and noise. Wing-loading values for nighttime hunters such as tawny, long-eared, barn, and boreal owls are among the lowest. These owls are also very silent fliers. Owls that hunt during daylight hours—snowy, burrowing, and northern hawk owls, for example—do not fly quite as stealthily. Instead, they have sacrificed silence for greater speed and power.

A great gray owl slips toward its prey on hushed wings. (Photo © by Jeff Lepore)

Barred owls are excellent hunters. They fly from place to place stealthily. When sitting still, their feather patterns allow them to blend with their surroundings. (Photo © by Gregory Scott)

Much of an owl's apparent size consists of airy contour and semiplume feathers. Owls in northern climates have downy feathers that insulate their legs, while temperate zone owls, such as barn and burrowing, have sparsely feathered legs. (Photo © by Connie Toops)

The feather patterns that conceal owls perched on a daytime roost, known as cryptic coloration, are important in hiding owls from both predators and prey. The long-eared owl is particularly masterful of camouflage posturing, so much so that humans can walk within a few feet of these birds without ever seeing them. As do many forest owls, long-eared owls perch near the trunk of a tree and do not flush easily when approached. If disturbed, a long-eared owl quietly draws itself into an elongated, upright stance with ear tufts erected, eyebrows spread, and rictal or "moustache" feathers pushed forward to hide the beak. Many owls raise the shoulder or wing to cover their highly visible throat patches. Most owls close their eyes so there is no focal point to draw the notice of a predator, although the long-eared owl usually keeps its amber eyes open. Even so, the net effect is an appearance much more like a stubby tree branch than a living bird. Feather patterns of screech and scops owls mimic mottled clumps of lichens on tree bark. In elon-

gated postures and holding quite still, owls are very difficult to detect.

An owl's coloration is not a reliable indicator of its age or sex. Scops and screech owls have both reddish and gray phases, but a pair in which one bird is rust-colored and the other gray does not mean one must be the female and the other the male. Adult male snowy owls are nearly pure white, while females and juveniles are flecked with dark barring. In most other species males and females have similar plumages. Young owls may be slightly darker than parents but they have similar color patterns. Exceptions are juvenile boreal and northern saw-whet owls, which have much darker breast feathers and facial discs than their parents.

In some species, coloration varies with the geographical area. Birds of open habitats—deserts, grasslands, or tundra—tend to be lighter than owls of the forest. Owls of coniferous forests are likely to be gray, while those of deciduous forests are more often brown.

Tiny hooks, called barbules, lock feathers together so they will support a bird in flight. Barbules on the leading edges of owl wing feathers are fringed to slice through the air silently. (Photo © by Connie Toops)

The broad, rounded shape of the little owl's wing is typical of most owls. This wing design allows owls to fly with a minimum of effort and noise. (Photo © by Stephen Dalton, Animals Animals)

Owls that dwell in coniferous forests tend to have gray tones in their plumage, while owls of deciduous forests are usually brown. (Photo © by Joe McDonald)

The process of natural selection favors colors that conceal the owls best. In every generation some individuals perish before they reproduce while others live long enough to bear offspring. Successful survivors pass traits to these offspring. Like human eye color, feather color is inherited.

For example, in eastern screech owls, genes for reddish plumage dominate over gray, as in humans genes for brown eyes are dominant over blue. Without the influence of natural selection, one would expect more rust-colored owls in any given population. A rusty screech owl blends well with the brown leaves lingering in a winter deciduous forest, and the rusty phase is more common in most of the eastern United States. But a reddish owl is more visible than a gray one against the drab bark of a pine or cypress tree. A more noticeable owl is likely to be targeted by a predator. Thus, it is not surprising that gray screech owls are more abundant in northern coniferous forests and in the lichen- and Spanish moss-draped cypress swamps of the Southeast. The western screech owl (*Otus kennicotti*), which primarily inhabits coniferous forests, is most abundant in the gray color phase.

Ruffed grouse also have gray and brown color phases, and the distribution of their color morphs is very similar to the distribution of gray and brown screech owls. Studies of the European scops owl show that the gray phase is often found resting close to the trunk of a tree while the reddish phase is likely to roost in the foliage.

Flammulated owls, whose Latin name means "flame-colored," migrate into the western mountains of the United States and southern British Columbia each summer. The secretive habits and cryptic coloration of these small owls make them one of the least-seen western species. Northern birds are grayer, while those of the southern United States and Mexico are burnished with rust-colored streaks. They blend remarkably with the red-brown trunks of the ponderosa pine forests in which they hunt. Northern and feruginous pygmy owls also have red and gray phases.

The majority of European tawny owls are brown, which makes sense in their deciduous woodland habitat. There is, however, a less common gray color form. Barn owl plumages do not vary with geography as much as other owls, although individuals range from immaculately white to a dark-breasted golden hue. At close range female barn owls can often be distinguished from males by the greater number of dark spots on their underparts.

Barn owls are the least cryptically colored of the owls in the Northern Hemisphere. Most forest-dwelling owls avoid notice while roosting in the open because their feathers blend with the patterns of tree bark or broken limbs. Barn owls tend to protect themselves from view during the daylight hours by roosting quietly inside hollow trees or buildings.

Owls invest long periods of time in raising their chicks. The musical courtship calls of tawny owls intensify as they proclaim territories in late winter. Five months later, the nearly grown youngsters will still be following their parents and begging for food. (Photo © by Robert Maier, Animals Animals)

RITES OF SPRING

The night was mild for mid-December in northeastern Mississippi. I had just settled into bed at a few minutes past ten o'clock when I heard a faint *whoo, hoo-hoo-hoo, whoo, whoo* outside. It is unusual for great horned owls to visit our suburban yard, so I got up and opened the window to listen. Again came the rising series of hoots, which sounded as though it originated in a small grove of cedars and hardwoods northwest of our fenceline. This time the calls were answered by a distant, mellow *hoo, hoo-hoo-oo, hoo, hoo* from a patch of pinewoods to the northeast. The closer owl continued to hoot, at intervals of one to several minutes, for half an hour. The distant owl answered two more times, then grew silent.

Just as humans recognize the voices of friends and relatives, so owls find other owl voices distinctive. Owls defend territories, the home ranges used for feeding and nesting, against others of their kind. Some owls also drive competing species away. The Ural owl, which is known in Sweden as *slaguggla* or "attacking owl," chases off or kills tawny owls that attempt to use nest sites within its territory.

The most efficient way for an owl to advertise the boundaries of its territory is to fly to various perches around the edges and hoot. Songs build invisible fences. Hooting contests do not involve competitors in physical combat, yet they advise intruders to stay away. In general, the owl that sings the loudest or persists the longest wins the territory. Among great horned owls, there is a vacant buffer zone or "no-owl's-land" between territories so that competitors do not accidentally stray onto one another's holdings.

Usually the male owl selects a territory and then calls to locate a mate. The voices of female owls are normally higher than males'. Unmated females attracted to a male's advertisements have distinct answering calls that allow them to enter his territory peacefully. Even in species normally active by day, territorial calling usually takes place at night. As courtship progresses, paired scops, little, barred, tawny, long-eared, and screech owls may sing vocal duets.

The voices of large owls, such as the eagle or snowy, carry a mile or more. Many owl songs are pitched from the A above middle C on a piano to about the midpoint of the sixth octave. Owls can hear these sounds well, although they are lower than the range of their best reception. Low sounds carry better through the forest and across meadows or marshy terrain.

Vocalizations are produced in the owl's syrinx, at the base of the windpipe. Here thin tissues form elastic membranes. Air from the lungs passes across these membranes and makes them vibrate. Tension on three sets of muscles attached to the membranes controls pitch.

In general, larger owls have lower calls and

smaller owls have vocalizations of higher frequencies. One exception is the diminutive flammulated owl, which has a very low song. Small owls usually have modestly sized territories, thus less powerful voices suffice. The flammulated owl, however, has a territory larger than other owls of its proportions. The low call is necessary to carry farther through the forest vegetation.

Owls sing a wide range of songs, some of which have been described in less-than-musical terms as whining, barking, and caterwauling. Blood-curdling screams serve as a chick protection signal for barn owls. Other species emit short, loud hoots to warn mates if danger approaches. Hoots are also given as part of the courting ritual.

Beak clicking, a sound made by snapping both parts of the bill together, is a defensive warning. This noise is commonly made by owls as hawks or crows fly overhead. It also accompanies a highly defensive posture of fanning wings and tail outward, crouching, stamping feet, and swaying the head back and forth while hissing. Owls do this if cornered to look as dangerous and sound as enraged as possible. In desperate attempts to defend themselves, threatened great horned owls will flip onto their backs and attack savagely with their talons.

In addition to audible signals, owls communicate by sight, even in low light conditions. Colors are unrecognizable in very dim light, but white throat markings such as those that puff out each time an eagle, great horned, or burrowing owl hoots, stand out in sharp contrast to gray or brown breast feathers. Light eyebrow and moustache markings, also visible at a distance, change an owl's appearance depending upon whether it is relaxed or alarmed. Many owls raise or lower ear tufts, transforming the shape of the head silhouette depending upon the bird's mood. Erect, elongated postures signal an owl's alarm, while more horizontal positions are typical of courtship.

During the nesting season most owls are faithful to just one mate. Occasionally male snowy,

barn, boreal, great gray, or northern hawk owls will care for two females at once. Species including spotted, barred, eagle, and little owls usually mate for life, with pairs occupying the same territory — and sometimes the same nest tree — for several years. Certain barn owl roosts have been observed under continuous occupation for seventy years, although not by the same owls. Barred owls have been reported occupying woodlots for up to thirty-five years, and little owls have nested in the same place for more than a quarter century. In these situations, when one owl dies, the mate takes a new partner into its territory. The male customarily remains in its original home range and calls to advertise his availability. Some widowed females stay put until a suitable replacement male wanders by, although others leave their former home in search of a mate.

Most owls begin to court at the end of their first year. Larger owls, such as the great horned and snowy, may not mate and raise chicks until their second summer.

For great gray owls, courtship begins while winter snows still blanket northern forests, sedge meadows, and tamarack bogs. Paired great gray owls nest in the same vicinity each year, but not always in the same tree. Male owls do not devour their prey as quickly as they would have in the fall, especially if a female is watching from a nearby perch. If the male captures a pocket gopher or other small rodent, he pauses for a moment while perched on a mossy hummock or lichen-covered log with the limp animal dangling from his beak.

The female, her attention riveted on the male, hoots in a soft tone that resembles the call of begging owlets. She shifts her weight from one leg to the other, leaning forward slightly in anticipation. The male flies to the female's branch and sidles closer. His smaller size is apparent as they sit side by side. He closes his eyes and dangles the lifeless prey within her reach. She grasps the rodent, utters a mewing sound, and swallows it. The pair bond is thus strengthened numerous times over the next few weeks as the male owl proves his hunting skills and feeds his mate.

As a bond of trust grows between the great

Owls advise intruders to stay away from their nests by hooting from perches along the edges of their territories. (Photo © by Gregory Scott)

grays, they show what seems to be genuine affection by grooming each other. Usually the male lands on a branch next to his mate and while facing her, nuzzles the feathers of her facial disc. As the female tilts forward, the male preens feathers on the top and back of her head. Then she returns the favor, gently nibbling and rubbing his face and head. The male may continue by carefully combing the female's breast feathers with his talons. The act of mating, which lasts only a few seconds, consummates this bonding.

In *The Great Gray Owl: Phantom of the Northern Forest*, Canadian owl expert Robert W. Nero shares this conjugal moment from the private lives of two great gray owls:

The male flew into a tree, where shortly he was joined by the female. At that point the birds were about three meters (20 feet) apart on the same branch. When the female flew, the male followed and, like a raven (Corvus corax), cupped his wings, braking and falling upon her in mid-air. He dropped onto the female for a second, then they separated and flew off together.

Although barn owls have seventeen call variations, several of which are used while courting, their mating ritual also includes bonding flights and feeding by the male. Courtship begins in earnest on the mild nights of late winter. Prospective mates may exchange short screeches of greeting after roosting separately during the day. Then they perform a paired flight in which the birds flutter back and forth chasing each other while uttering a series of rapid squeaking and clicking sounds.

The male barn owl displays to the female in "moth flight," a hovering exposé of his white underwings. This is sometimes climaxed by clapping his wings together with a soft, whooshing "poof." Then the male will suddenly dash into the barn or other area where he intends for the female to nest. She often follows, calling in a soft "snore" very similar to the sound young owls use to beg. This triggers the male to present food, which he does by passing a dead rodent from his bill to the female's. She bows forward while he mounts and nibbles at the feathers on her neck. Barn owls are extremely skittish while nesting

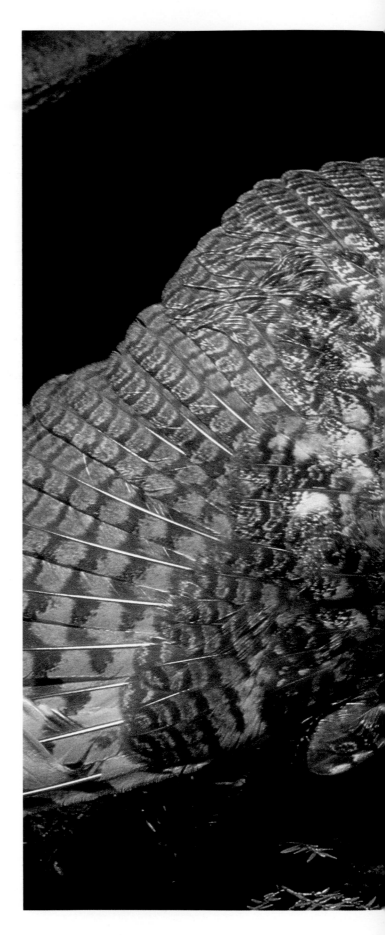

When faced with danger, owls such as this long-eared try to look as large and threatening as possible. They spread their wings and hiss menacingly. (Photo © by Breck Kent)

Like many species, spotted owls are faithful to just one mate. The male strengthens his bond with the female by bringing food throughout courtship and nesting periods. (Photo © by Norman Barrett, courtesy USDA Forest Service)

and tending young chicks. Unexpected interruptions by human observers during this period may incite adults to give horrendous screeches if their nest is approached. On rare occasions barn owls roost inside rotting trees infected with phosphorescent fungi. The material saturates the bird's wings so that they emit a ghostly greenish glow as they fly. Through the centuries, human encounters with these sights and sounds have led to the association of barn owls with tales of winged devils.

Mutual preening of feathers on the neck, face, and back of the head is practiced by many owls as a bonding ritual. The bird being preened relaxes, often twitters, and seems to enjoy the experience. Handlers of captive owls state that their birds respond favorably to head scratching. Researchers working with wild owls mention that a few great gray and spotted owls have gently nibbled their hair as the unsuspecting scientists bent the tops of their heads toward the owls. Among owls, this behavior probably reduces aggression between larger female and smaller male owls.

Without exception, female owls are larger than their mates. The differences in size are most pronounced in species including the eagle, great horned, great gray, snowy, spotted, barred, tawny, and boreal owls. This is a trait common to raptors. Female sharp-shinned hawks weigh 75 percent more than their mates. Female peregrines and gyrfalcons are 55 percent heavier, while Cooper's hawks outweigh their mates by 60 percent.

From a reproductive viewpoint, this sexual dimorphism makes sense. Most owls begin nesting during the winter months. In order to brood eggs through bitter winter storms, female owls must be large enough to generate abundant body heat. Entering the breeding period with a larger body and more food reserves also helps the fe-

Most owls have only one brood per year. Great horned owls usually lay two or three eggs, but in years when rodents are especially abundant, they produce larger clutches. (Photo © by Scott Sharkey)

male endure the stresses of the long nesting season.

With few exceptions, the female owl does all of the incubating and brooding. For the six to eight weeks the female is confined to the nest, the male brings her food. She leaves the nest unattended for only a few minutes each day while she drinks water or attends to her toilet. A large female seems quite able to dominate a smaller male without physical struggles into fulfilling her needs during this critical period.

Some ornithologists theorize that male owls, being smaller and more agile, are actually more efficient at catching prey than are the larger females. Rodents usually outnumber other mammals. Small male owls hunting rodents can often provide more food for the mother and nestlings in a quick series of catches than could a big male owl waiting longer periods for larger prey.

Male and female barn, long-eared, short-eared, burrowing, and little owls are much closer to the same size. Sexual dimorphism is least pro-nounced in the small, insect-eating owls. It is probably not a coincidence that similar-sized insectivorous owls spend less time hunting than do highly dimorphic owls that eat birds and larger mammals.

Owls that build their own nests are exceptional. Burrowing owls are capable of digging underground lairs, but usually they appropriate abandoned badger, prairie dog, or gopher tortoise tunnels. Barn owls have been known to excavate dens in the soft soil of stream banks and road cuts. Many of the small owls rely on abandoned woodpecker holes. Larger owls nest in hollow sections of broken treetops and vacant hawk, crow, or squirrel nests. These birds may rearrange existing twigs or wood chips but do not add new nest material except for the incidental feathers dropped by the female as she preens. Barn owls do regurgitate pellets at the nest and

Baby owls hatch at one- to three-day intervals. The older chicks grab food first, and in years of prey scarcity, only these stronger siblings survive. (Photo © by Scott Sharkey)

use them to cushion their white, elliptical eggs.

Short-eared and snowy owls, both of which reproduce on the ground in open terrain, make nest scrapes. Snowies choose a raised hummock while short-eared owls usually situate their nests in the shelter of grasses or shrubs. Both scratch a shallow depression to hold the eggs. These depressions are thinly lined with pieces of grass, stubble, and scattered feathers.

Owls invest a long time in raising chicks. Great horned owls, which lay eggs in January (south) to late February (north), require ten weeks for their young to fledge. Once they learn to fly, the juveniles are still not independent of their parents. It takes another two or three months for the babies to acquire skills that allow them to swoop noiselessly onto unsuspecting prey at night. In the meantime, they follow the parents and beg for food.

In the far north, owls do not have the luxury of a lengthy summer to raise young. They do have long periods of daylight in the late spring, so nesting and chick-rearing are timed to coincide with maximum prey availability. Most owl species raise only one brood per year. In the northern portions of their ranges, owls telescope nesting activities into shorter but more concentrated periods. Only barn owls, which inhabit temperate and tropical climates, raise two or three broods a year.

Unlike ducks and geese that deposit all of their eggs before beginning to incubate them, owls warm their eggs from the time they are laid. Since eggs arrive at one- to three-day intervals, a clutch of six owlets will look like stairsteps, with chicks from two weeks to two days old by the time the last egg hatches. This is a good reproductive strategy for predators such as owls, which may be faced with seasons of scarce prey.

Even in years of abundant rodents, the older, stronger chicks grab their share first. Weaker

Great horned owls feed their chicks for about four months until the young birds gain enough skills to hunt on their own. The chick-feeding period coincides with seasons when prey is most plentiful. (Photo © by Scott Sharkey)

Several weeks before they can fly, great horned owlets clamber on branches near the nest tree. (Photo © by Michael Quinton)

Young owls may jump from the nest before their wings will support flight. Usually the parents stay close enough to swoop in and protect the rambunctious youngsters from danger. (Photo © by Steven Faccio)

64

chicks eat only when older siblings are full. In times of prey scarcity, just the older chicks survive. After a day or two without food, the youngest birds weaken and fail to beg. In the case of snowy, great gray, and barn owls—and probably other species as well—the small dead chicks may eventually be eaten by the older nestmates. Thus in lean times, when little prey is available, only a few chicks survive. Their success is aided by the reduced competition of the youngest siblings. In these years if all chicks had hatched together, the parents might not have fed them sufficiently and perhaps none would have received enough nutrition to reach adulthood.

Usually the male owl brings food near the nest but does not directly feed the chicks. The female either calls when she spies the male, coaxing him to deliver the meal to her, or she flies to him and receives the prey. She takes it back to the nest and will pull off chunks of meat for newly hatched chicks. As soon as they are capable, babies gobble down whole prey.

The chicks are blind and sparsely covered with down when first born. Mother owl gathers them next to the brood patch beneath her fluffy breast feathers, enclosing them on each side with drooping wings. The young birds grow and feather rapidly and can soon stay warm on their own. From then on the female stands nearby, ready to shield them from the view of passing crows and hawks or from hot sun or rain by spreading her wings over them.

Birds that mature inside tree cavities, namely the little, boreal, screech, elf, saw-whet, hawk, and pygmy owls, tend to remain hidden inside until ready to fly. The young of these species have white V markings above the beak and light moustaches beside it, presumably to guide the attending parent to correct placement of food when peering into the dark cavity.

Chicks of platform-nesting owls are much more restless. Long before they develop flight skills, they begin "branching," a term that describes their acrobatic explorations of the nest tree. Using beaks and talons, they grasp bark and twigs, pulling themselves up the trunk or onto new branches.

"Orphaned" great horned owlets are usually rambunctious youngsters who hop out of the nest before their wings will support flight. Parents may coax these young explorers into a nearby tree. Some species, including the great gray and Ural. will attack humans or other animals that threaten their youngsters. Should you ever find a young owl, the best response is to keep pet dogs and cats away and watch from a distance. If parents do not rescue the orphans within several hours, call your local game warden to attend to them.

In addition to dive bombing humans, raccoons, martens, or other nest invaders, adult owls sometimes feign injuries to distract potential predators. As a human approaches the nest of a great horned owl, the male has been reported to circle above the invader to attract attention. If the nest is very near, the male dives, actually crashing into the ground. It rolls onto its back, spreads its wings, and pretends to be severely injured. In similar situations, adult long-eared owls may plunge to the base of their nest tree. They pretend to drag themselves away on feebly beating wings. Once they lead the intruder from the nest, they fly off.

Great Gray Owl Courtship: *Male great gray owls begin to establish territories in mid-February. They perch near a potential nest site and call in a series of low hoots to advertise for a mate. Once the male captures a female's fancy, he catches voles, pocket gophers, and other rodent prey to present to her. This attentive care proves the male's skills as a hunter and at the same time nourishes the female for the weeks ahead that she will spend confined to the nest. (Photo © by Michael Quinton)*

Great Gray Owl Courtship: *As the bond of trust between the great gray owls grows, the smaller male approaches his larger mate with less apprehension. They seem to show genuine affection by nuzzling and preening each other. (Photo © by Michael Quinton)*

Great Gray Owl Courtship: *Great gray owls raise their chicks in broken-topped snags or abandoned hawk nests. The female lays three to five eggs and once incubation begins, she seldom leaves the nest. The eggs hatch in about a month, and the female feeds the chicks at first by gently tearing off bite-sized bits of prey. Soon the chicks are large enough to swallow whole voles or pocket gophers. (Photo © by Jeff Foott)*

Great Gray Owl Courtship: *The male great gray owl brings a steady supply of food to his mate and the youngsters. Usually, the male passes his catch to the female rather than directly feeding the newly hatched chicks. (Photo © by Michael Quinton)*

Great Gray Owl Courtship: *The female great gray gathers her young chicks against her brood patch to insulate them from the cold. Eventually, the owlets develop enough feathers to stay warm on their own. Then the mother owl shifts to a perch beside the nest or on a nearby branch. She returns to spread her wings over the young birds during inclement weather or to shield them from view of predators such as great horned owls, ravens, and hawks. (Photo © by Jeff Foott)*

At Corkscrew Swamp, in a tree not twenty feet away, sat a pair of barred owls. They watched me curiously for a few moments, then flew. (Photo © by Connie Toops)

AT HOME IN FORESTS AND FENS

Dusk fell over Corkscrew Swamp, an Audubon sanctuary in southern Florida. The cypress trees in leafless winter garb stood stark against the golden horizon. I strolled along the boardwalk, stopping now and then to gaze into pools of clear, dark water below. Although I was the only person on the trail this evening, I had the distinct feeling I was being watched. I scanned the branches overhead and finally discovered a barred owl sitting about fifteen yards away. Its dark eyes followed my every move.

Now that I was peering back, the owl ruffled its feathers and looked away. It stretched a wing and then nibbled at plumage on its shoulder. Periodically it glanced in my direction. After ten minutes of half-hearted preening, it yawned and allowed its eyelids to droop. The sweet notes of a whip-poor-will echoed across the swamp as the last rays of the setting sun transformed the western sky into a fleeting blaze of orange.

Whoo-who-hoo-hoo. Who-who-hoo-hoo-all, the melodic call of a distant barred owl drifted through the humid air. My owl was now wide awake and staring in the direction of this sound. The next moment, it lifted silently from the branch, moving like a shadow among the lichen-covered cypress trunks. A mockingbird scolded. Seconds later the owl was out of sight.

I shouldered my camera and tripod and continued along the boardwalk. Frogs and crickets chirped their evening songs. When I reached the edge of the cypresses, I paused to watch some dragonflies darting back and forth over the marsh. For some unexplained reason, I turned to look over my shoulder. There, in a tree not twenty feet away, sat both owls. They, too, were watching for insects, birds settling onto night roosts, cotton rats, or marsh rabbits. For these owls, the hunt was just beginning. They regarded me curiously for a few moments, then one followed the other on whispering wings into the nearby pine forest. Half an hour later I heard them hooting softly to each other. In the light of the rising moon, I saw silhouettes of their rounded wings. The owls cruised into the open, snatched hummingbird-sized moths in midair, and returned to a pine branch to consume them.

Barred owls, round-headed in silhouette with mottled brown and white plumage, range across the eastern United States and southern Canada. They are most abundant in wetland habitats. Cypress swamps of the Southeast—Okeefenokee, Atchafalaya, Congaree, and many smaller fens—ring with the haunting calls of barred owls. Most of the tree islands in the Florida Everglades have a resident pair.

Barred owls are food generalists, opportunistic birds that prey on mouse- to rabbit-sized mammals, songbirds, frogs, snakes, lizards, crayfish, large insects, and fish. They use hollow trees as well as abandoned hawk, crow, and squirrel

Barred owls are most abundant in wetland habitat such as the cypress swamps of the southeastern United States. (Photo © by Connie Toops)

Spotted owls resemble barred and tawny owls in size and appearance. Spotted owls live in old-growth western forests, where they hunt flying squirrels, wood rats, and red-backed voles. (Photo © by Norman Barrett, courtesy USDA Forest Service)

nests in which to raise their young.

Like barred owls, tawny owls are successful generalists. Tawny owls occupy a variety of habitats, ranging from wooded city parks in London to vast coniferous forest plantations, as long as mature trees are in ample supply. Tawny owls seek out natural cavities in these old trees and in cliff ledges, and use abandoned nests of crows, buzzards, magpies, and squirrels. Tawny owls are more strictly nocturnal than barred owls, relying on hearing to capture prey and on an excellent memory of the trees and obstacles in their home range to avoid bumping into them while hunting on the darkest of nights. Tawny owl prey includes mice, voles, small rabbits, birds, frogs, insects, and earthworms.

Spotted owls, which outwardly resemble their relatives the barred and tawny owls in size and appearance, have much different requirements. Spotted owls dwell primarily in mature forests of the American West. Spotted owls of the Pacific Coast inhabit centuries-old forests dominated by Sitka spruce or Douglas fir. Some of the trees are two hundred feet tall, but the owls nest in shorter snags with hollow, rotten tops. They hunt over huge territories of as much as 2,000 acres of mossy understory. Usually spotted owls return to the same tree each year to raise young. These night-hunters sit on branches and watch for flying squirrels, voles, and deer mice, which they then pounce upon.

A separate subspecies of the spotted owl lives in woodlands at the bottoms of cool, moist canyons in Colorado, New Mexico, Arizona, and Mexico. Like spotted owls of the Pacific Northwest, they rest in shady forests by day and hunt at night. Their earthy brown plumage dappled with white resembles the patterns of sunlight filtering through branches. Sitting still near the trunk of a tree, they are difficult to see. In the southern Rockies, wood rats replace flying squirrels as a major item in the spotted owl's diet. Spotted owls in California regularly catch arboreal red-backed voles.

Recent studies suggest that large prey animals, such as rats and flying squirrels, are foods important to successful breeding and reproduction. As logging claims old-growth tracts in the Pacific Northwest, spotted owls are forced into less suitable hunting habitats and find fewer flying squirrels. Their poor ability to adapt to other food sources may be partially responsible for recent declines in the numbers of spotted owls.

When faced with seasonal shortages of favorite foods, other sedentary owls such as the barred, eagle, and tawny simply eat more of something else. As generalists, they can capture and eat a variety of prey depending on what is plentiful at the time. Several of the smaller owls, including elf, flammulated, and scops, migrate north in spring to take advantage of seasonally abundant insects. Flammulated owls actually follow a different autumn return route, remaining at higher elevations and traveling at a more leisurely pace because they are catching large moths in the mountains at summer's end. Long-eared, short-eared, and saw-whet owls migrate south to ride out inclement weather in the midlatitudes. They fly back north to capitalize on summer's abundance. By migrating, they experience less competition for voles, mice, and nesting songbirds than they would by remaining in the same area year-round.

During years of vole shortages in Scandinavia, observers in the Fair Isles have noted visits by small flocks of long-eared and short-eared owls. Although owls are not usually thought of as traveling in flocks, groups of migrant long-eared owls are seen in April and again in late October or early November passing the Shetland Islands, along the northeast coast of Great Britain, on the Baltic coast, and crossing Swiss mountain passes. Some of these birds winter in central Europe, while others continue southeast to Syria, Turkey, Iran, and Iraq. There, as well as in the United States, long-eared owls gather each winter in groups of half a dozen or more at favorite roosting thickets. Long-eared owls banded in Saskatchewan and Michigan have wintered in central Mexico and a burrowing owl ringed in Utah was later found on the Baja Peninsula in western Mexico. A snowy owl banded in Cambridge Bay, Canada, migrated 3,500 miles, where it was discovered in Sakhalin, U.S.S.R.

Great gray, snowy, and northern hawk owls have close ties with the prey animals of their northern habitats. Expanses of tundra and taiga forests have less species diversity than southern areas. In favorable seasons, however, the long summer days can be incredibly productive.

Northern owls prey heavily on voles and lemmings. Lemmings are plump, short-tailed arctic rodents about twice the size of a house mouse. Voles are smaller and mouselike in appearance. Both live in underground tunnels and are active throughout the winter.

Voles and lemmings normally live only one to three years. In mild seasons they make up for short life spans by producing up to six offspring in each of their four or five litters. In back-to-back mild years, one pair may increase to fifty individuals. If the weather should be bountiful three years in succession, the ground seethes with their tunnels, and the little animals scurry about looking for new sources of food.

Northern owls prosper during rodent bonanzas. When lemmings and voles are abundant, male owls bring more food to their mates. Well-nourished females lay larger clutches of eggs. In these years of high rodent populations, there is plenty of food to rear the entire brood.

Vole and lemming population explosions are not uniform throughout the Arctic. Rodents may be at normal levels in one region while several hundred miles away, numbers increase exponentially. Many northern owls are nomadic and follow these peaks. They nest where prey is plentiful, sometimes very near each other. In times of abundance, great gray owls, for instance, hunt among themselves and other kinds of owls without the territorial aggression observed in leaner years.

If voles and lemmings reproduce abundantly for several years in a row, they begin to crowd themselves so severely that food sources are exhausted. Many of the little creatures starve, and others die trying to cross mountains, lakes, or

Long-eared owls migrate south to spend the winter in milder climates. Small groups of these well-camouflaged birds often roost together in thickets or dense conifers. (Photo © by Gary Meszaros)

Northern owls, such as the snowy, prosper in years when lemmings and voles are abundant. When prey populations crash, these owls appear in great numbers far south of their normal breeding range. (Photo © by Thomas Mangelson)

Lemmings, which are about twice the size of house mice, make up for short life spans by producing up to two dozen offspring in a good season. (Photo © by Maslowski Wildlife Productions)

snowfields in search of new feeding grounds. In the meantime, opportunistic predators such as owls, jaegers, skuas, hawks, and arctic foxes have gathered to feast on the bounty. Finally, vole and lemming populations crash, an occurrence that takes place every third or fourth year. Only a few individuals survive to start the reproductive cycle once more.

Northern owl populations increase in response to rodent peaks. When an abundant food source gives out, owls and their offspring wander across many miles of tundra or taiga searching for alternate sources. They may find another region where voles and lemmings are abundant. Snowy owls will target other prey, such as birds and arctic hares. But hare populations peak and crash as well. Sometimes there simply is not enough food left in the high north to support the owls living there. In normal years large numbers of snowy, great gray, and northern hawk owls winter in the north. In times of scarcity, however, they may wander south of their breeding range in search of food.

Usually the immature birds leave first. It is normal for young owls to venture out on their own by autumn, and it is not unusual for first-year birds to travel quite far from their nesting area. Unfortunately, young owls suffer the highest mortality. They may be hungry when they part company with their parents, and finding new sources of food can be difficult. Many inexperienced birds are injured or killed in accidents with unfamiliar objects such as power lines and motor vehicles.

Ecologically, it makes sense for the young to leave first. In some years there is enough food left in the north to support the more experienced parents. At winter's end, they will be ready to nest anew without making a long migratory flight. The outcast young also benefit. In times of scarcity, they would likely die by remaining. They also would reduce the food available to their parents. By flying south, they may find milder weather and more dependable food sources. Some will undoubtedly survive and return the following year to breed.

Female boreal owls fly south before the males, who remain to guard the nesting territory as long as they can. When the icy crust on freezing and thawing snow cover becomes too hard to crash through, the males leave also. If winter food supplies fail completely, large influxes of both juvenile and adult owls are observed migrating to milder climes. These irregular mass movements are known as irruptions. For great gray, boreal, and northern hawk owls, they occur at three- to five-year intervals, linked with rodent cycles. Northern owl species do not always irrupt together. Although some snowy owls may migrate south each winter, major invasions of the white owls occur in years of combined rodent and hare failures.

From January through April 1979, the largest owl invasion of the century was recorded in eastern Canada and New England. For example, Amherst Island, a twenty-three-square-mile landmass in the midst of Lake Ontario, was temporary home to three dozen great gray, a dozen snowy, and two dozen each of long-eared and short-eared owls. Six other species were observed in smaller numbers. The previous winter saw numerous boreal and great gray owls west of Lake Superior. In 1983 and 1984 season, hundreds of great gray owls wintered in the lake regions of Minnesota, Ontario, and Quebec.

These invasions are bonanzas for birders, when "most wanted" (and usually most elusive) species such as great gray, boreal, and northern hawk owls perch on highway billboards and farm fences. The owls are unwary and can be viewed at very close range.

Snowy owls naturally attract attention because of their large size and elegant white plumage. While many invade grassy wildlife refuges and seashores on the coast of the northeastern United States, they have also been observed sitting near airport runways or on the roofs of urban shopping malls. A few years ago a snowy owl was observed in the District of Columbia, on the Mall near the Washington Monument, then on the roof of the Senate Office Building.

Owl watchers never forget the excitement of seeing these unusual and magnificent birds in irruptive years. While in college in Ohio, my husband and I heard of a snowy owl that had taken up winter residence in a cornfield next to an interstate highway north of Dayton. The following weekend, we drove the seventy-five miles from school to the site. Sure enough, sitting in the middle of the stubble field, like a chip from an arctic glacier, was the owl. We studied it at length through our binoculars, thrilling each time the bird turned its head to stare at us with its golden eyes.

That field is now part of an industrial park. On my occasional trips back to Ohio, I pass the spot. Although the scene has changed, I always pause and visualize the owl that for a brief time brought a bit of the high north into our lives.

Nesting Snowy Owls: *Snowy owls nest on the tundra, frequently near a pond or stream. The paired birds scrape a shallow depression in the soil and line it with grass or moss. The nest is usually situated in a place with a good view so the owls can watch for predators such as arctic foxes. (Photo © by Maslowski Wildlife Productions)*

Nesting Snowy Owls: *Once the female snowy owl begins to brood the eggs, she seldom leaves the nest. Incubation takes about a month, and thereafter the chicks hatch at two-day intervals. The first babies are about two weeks old by the time the last nestling appears. The female tears off bits of prey and gently feeds the small nestlings. She shelters them beneath her, against her warm brood patch, to fend off the chill of the damp ground. (Photo © by Maslowski Wildlife Productions)*

Nesting Snowy Owls: *At five days of age, the chicks open their eyes. They are covered first with fine, white down. By two weeks, the chicks have thicker gray down and their wing feathers are beginning to develop. Now they can swallow lemmings whole, and they usually consume a couple of the chubby rodents each day. (Photo © by Maslowski Wildlife Productions)*

Nesting Snowy Owls: *The male does all of the hunting for his mate and the young chicks. He delivers lemmings, birds, trout, and hares, hunting mostly during the low light of dusk and dawn. If the female cannot use all of the food he brings, she will cache it near the nest. In this photo the white owl is returning to its mate with a freshly killed common eider. (Photo © by Maslowski Wildlife Productions)*

Great horned owls prey on a variety of animals, from robin-sized songbirds, to skunks, to the young of other owls. Songbirds recognize owls as a threat and gather around them in scolding, chattering mobs. (Photo © by Maslowski Wildlife Productions)

RAPTOR RIVALS

Although owls and hawks belong to unrelated orders, or categories, in the classification of birds, they both fulfill roles as raptors, or birds of prey. The word "raptor" comes from the Latin language. Its meaning, "plundering or taking by force," reveals the long tradition of human hostility toward these birds. Throughout history raptors, which eat mammals and game birds such as ducks and grouse, have been viewed as competitors for human foods.

Even though owls and hawks evolved separately, they possess similar equipment for hunting. Both have large, powerful feet tipped with sharp talons. Owls catch and stun prey with their feet. Another interpretation of the Latin origin for "raptor" means "to grip." Owls have reversible fourth toes, as do ospreys. This thumblike advantage allows owls to grasp and carry heavy prey. Owls and hawks rely on powerful wings to transport prey back to the nest. Sometimes these broad wings are used to mantle, or shield, prey from view. Raptors with hooked beaks use them to deliver a death blow to their prey, usually by biting the lower skull or neck area. Both hawks and owls disgorge undigested hair, bones, and feathers in castings called pellets.

Since hawks and owls are similar in so many ways, do they compete with one another? To some extent, yes, but they minimize this problem by a number of strategies, including varying times of hunting activity. Hawks are active during the day, while most owls feed between dusk and dawn. Interestingly, in the Hawaiian archipelago, short-eared owls do not encounter competition from hawks, except on the Big Island. Hawaiian owls, locally called *pueo*, fill a vacant ecological niche created by the absence of hawks and are quite active during the day.

The northern hawk owl, which is the most hawklike of the order, has long, tapered wings and tail. It hunts by day, using a hovering technique similar to that of small falcons. During the summer, when food is abundant, the hawk owl shares its boreal abode with merlins and American kestrels in Alaska and Canada. In Europe it experiences a summer influx of merlins, Eurasian kestrels, and European sparrowhawks. When food becomes more scarce in winter, the hawks migrate south but hawk owls remain.

Other strategies for reducing competition between hawks and owls are: eating different types of prey, nesting at different times, and choosing different nesting sites. But competition does take place.

Great gray owls and goshawks can come into conflict during the nesting season because they have similar nest site preferences. Both species inhabit spruce or pine forests with bogs and marshes interspersed. Great gray owls do not build nests, choosing instead the hollow tops of large snags, tangled growths of mistletoe, or twig nests constructed by ravens and various hawks. Since goshawk nests are already within preferred great gray habitat, these sprawling platforms are logical nest choices for the owls. Great gray owls readily appropriate abandoned goshawk aeries. Should the original owners return, great gray owls have been observed claiming their new homes by spreading their wings and ruffling their plumage in a threat display while perched in the midst of the nest.

Other species of owls apparently are less successful in keeping possession of usurped nests. In Scandinavia in 1971, researcher Kauko Huhtala discovered a goshawk nest with the hawk brooding three of its own eggs and one of a Ural owl. The owl hatched, but it was not tended well and eventually died. Early in this century, Dr. Louis Bishop documented a red-shouldered hawk nest in a woodlot near New Haven, Connecticut, that contained three hawk eggs, one barred owl egg, and an incubating barred owl. The following year he found the nest with two hawk eggs, one owl egg, and the hawk incubating. Throughout the eastern United States barred owls and red-shouldered hawks share the same swamps and forests with minimal aggression. Both species in the same nest, however, is most unusual.

Short-eared owls are birds of seashores, prairies, and marshes, and they feed primarily on voles living in these grasslands. They begin hunting in late afternoon, coursing low over the grasses in a flapping-gliding flight reminiscent of the northern harrier. Like harriers, the owls will hover over a particular spot before dropping feet-first onto a victim.

Short-eared owls sometimes nab songbirds on the wing. They also flush and harass ducks, herons, and gulls, though these birds are too large to be considered normal prey. Short-eared owls, which are capable of skilled aerial courtship displays, are also winged pirates. In the British Isles observers have witnessed short-eared owls stealing prey from both kestrels and stoats (ermines). On other occasions harriers and kestrels have bullied food caught by short-eared owls. Ravens also mob short-eared owls and carrion crows rob their nests.

Since short-eared owls and harriers are likely to be coursing over the same marshes in late af-ternoon, their encounters are of interest. A. C. Bent cites such an engagement in *Life Histories of North American Birds of Prey*:

The Owl pursued the Hawk, flying above the retreating bird. Hovering some ten feet above the Hawk, the Owl would suddenly swoop down in a fierce attack. In the same instant the Hawk would half turn like a tumbler pigeon, in such a manner as to strike the Owl with its talons as the bird passed. The dexterity and maneuver of the two birds was amazing. The attack was repeated seven or eight times. It is supposed the Hawk disturbed the Owl's nest and was being driven away.

Heimo Mikkola in *Owls of Europe* recorded 748 hawks killed by owls and 752 owls dispatched by hawks and eagles. He also cited 1,363 instances of owls slain by other owls, documenting competition among the species. Eagle owls are least tolerant. They regularly kill long-eared, short-eared, tawny, little, and boreal owls. The North American counterpart, the great horned owl, preys upon long-eared, barred, barn, and screech owls.

Tawny owls feed on scops owls where the two species inhabit the same regions of central Europe during the breeding season. Tawny owls also eat boreal owls and compete with Ural owls for cavities and nest sites in broken-topped trees. Ural owls are larger and more aggressive, however, killing or driving the tawny owls out of their territories. Great gray and northern hawk owls, on the other hand, are fairly tolerant of other owls nesting nearby.

Owls reduce competition for food among themselves in the same ways they avoid competing with hawks. Short-eared and long-eared owls share a preference for voles. Short-eared owls hunt them in the late afternoon and evening, while long-eared owls are nocturnal. The three most similar European owls are the great gray, tawny, and Ural. The great gray hunts mostly by day and is adept at survival in cold climates, using quick plunges and long talons to catch rodents under the snow. Nocturnal tawny owls, which choose more temperate hunting and nesting habitats, use their short, curved claws to

The northern hawk owl has a long, tapered tail and wings, suggestive of hawks. It hunts by day, using a hovering technique similar to that of small falcons. (Photo © by Gary Meszaros)

Because they are raptors, screech owls possess sharp beaks and strong talons. This enables them to capture prey ranging from frogs and insects to birds nearly as large as themselves. (Photo © by Cornell Laboratory of Ornithology)

Crows harass owls whenever the opportunity arises. (Photo © by Arthur Morris, Vireo)

Songbirds comprise a considerable part of a pygmy owl's diet. In the coniferous forests of Idaho, this northern pygmy owl feasts on an evening grosbeak. (Photo © by Charles Schwartz)

grab a variety of small mammals and birds. Ural owls hunt in both daylight and darkness. They are larger, tougher birds than tawny owls and use thicker claws to scoop up large prey such as rats, squirrels, and hares in addition to their more common diet of voles, shrews, and mice.

Owls also have interesting and complex relationships with other birds. Although barn owls occasionally eat smaller birds, their nest sites have at times been shared peacefully by house sparrows, doves, and kestrels. Many of the small- and medium-sized owls appropriate old woodpecker nests as their own. Flickers make

cavities of a perfect size for screech owls. But to hold claim to these dens, screech owls must occupy them early and continuously. Should a flicker return to a former nest that has a screech owl inside, the maker will not enter. If the owl leaves, the flicker may dart in, eject the owl's eggs, and guard against owl reentry by poking its formidable beak out of the hole. North American boreal owls also find flicker holes to their liking, while European boreal owls often rely on nests hollowed by crow-sized black woodpeckers.

Pygmy, screech, northern hawk, and tawny owls capture songbirds as a considerable part of their diets. Small birds recognize them as a threat, or at least it would seem so by their reactions. Titmice, chickadees, jays, blackbirds, and war-

Viewed from the perspective of a vole, the great gray owl is a formidable predator. (Photo © by Jeff Lepore)

blers gather around owls, chattering and scolding. Owls that are agile enough to pluck sleeping birds from their perches at night are usually too slow or reluctant to retaliate by day. Instead, they ruffle their feathers and snap their beaks at the raiders. Should the belligerent songsters dive close, a beleaguered owl may retreat into a tree cavity. If there is no escape, the owl will draw itself up into the vertical camouflage posture, close its eyes, and try to look like a stump. Eventually the noisy mob may lose interest and leave.

On both continents members of the crow family harass owls whenever the opportunity arises. Perhaps this is because corvids recognize owls as predators, especially of their nestlings. Whatever the reason, crows, ravens, magpies, and jays scream warning calls when they see owls and dive at them in flight. Their frenzied voices often recruit other corvids from neighboring territories to join in the torment.

The crow's attraction to owls has been used by hunters. Decoys and tethered live owls were traditionally set out to draw crows into gunning range. In Europe, falcons, buzzards, and accipiters dive-bomb their enemy the eagle owl. For years this method of live-baiting was used to kill the hawks. Now that we realize raptors are valued members of the ecological community, this practice has passed from favor and is illegal in most locations.

SHARING OUR WORLD WITH OWLS

"Owls Against City Rats" reads a headline in the news section of a recent gardening magazine. The accompanying article explains that the New York City Parks Department has stopped setting out poison baits for rats. Instead workers erected twenty-five wooden nest boxes in Forest, Prospect, Cunningham, and Central parks. The goal of "Operation Owl Prowl" is to attract resident barn owls. The owls will snooze in the boxes by day. At night they will emerge to feed in grasslands within the parks or on the grassy banks of the nearby East and Hudson rivers or Jamaica Bay.

Barn owls were successful on their own long before humans built barns, church steeples, and nest boxes. They nested in holes in rock cliffs, burrows along stream banks, hollow trees, and abandoned crows' nests. But as lofts, attics, mine shafts, granaries, and cisterns became available, barn owls moved in, gaining better protection from the weather and from predators. The owls are quiet and retiring during the day and usually very silent when entering and leaving the roost. This allows them to go almost unnoticed by humans, even in densely populated areas.

Barn owls were among the few native species of wildlife that benefited by the settling and clearing of the American Midwest. In 1879 Dr. John Wheaton, a pioneer naturalist in Ohio, wrote that only half a dozen barn owls had ever been recorded in the state. As trees were cut and land cleared for pastures in the 1920s and 1930s, barn owl populations increased rapidly. By the 1960s, however, ornithologists noted a sharp drop in barn owl numbers. In 1982 only two pairs were known to nest in Ohio. The barn owl is now listed as an endangered species throughout the Midwest. Scientists were puzzled by this decline, especially since the owls were doing well along the East Coast and in the southwestern United States.

The decline coincided with steel-sided barns replacing wooden ones, the boarding-up or removal of old country schools, and the disappearance of steeples and cupolas from modern architecture. "Perhaps there aren't enough nest sites," wildlife officials thought. They encouraged rural residents to install nest boxes on metal barns and granaries.

The Iowa Conservation Department released 250 captive-reared barn owls in the early 1980s. The Raptor Rehabilitation and Propagation Project released 500 barn owls in Missouri between 1979 and 1986. These efforts, however, failed to establish or increase barn owl populations.

Attracting barn owls to nest boxes has not been as easy as the successful bluebird nest box campaign. Bluebirds returned quickly and reproduced well because their insect food sources were still available. For bluebirds, the missing link was tree cavities, which are now provided by nest boxes. The missing link for barn owls, however, is food. Further studies revealed that barn owls in the Midwest prey on meadow voles. Meadow voles, in turn, depend upon dense stands of grasses in damp pastures and marshes. Voles make little runways through the grasses. They bustle along the trails both day

Although barn owls nest in attics, lofts, belfries, and warehouses, their nocturnal habits allow them to go unnoticed by many of their human neighbors. (Photo © by Dan Dreyfus)

Screech owls adapt well to suburban life. While screech owls readily accept nest boxes, they have also raised chicks in mailboxes, stovepipes, and even vacant apartments in martin houses. (Photo © by Joe McDonald)

Tawny owls often live in urban settings where large trees are plentiful. (Photo © by Stephen Dalton, Animals Animals)

and night, stopping to nibble plant stems. Too many of today's farms lack grassland habitats such as hayfields, meadows, and stream edges that provide ideal vole homes. If a barn owl cannot find enough food within a mile or two of the box, it will not nest.

According to barn owl expert Bruce Colvin, if Operation Owl Prowl is intended to control rats in New York City, money spent on the nest boxes would be more soundly invested in better trash cans. Although rats are abundant in the city streets near the owl roosts, Colvin's studies show city rats make up only a small percentage of barn owl diets. Animals the size of adult Norway rats are too large for barn owls to tackle. While barn owls will occasionally catch juvenile rats, they normally eat voles, which are about half the size of rats.

As a wildlife habitat enhancement project, however, the barn owls are excellent ambassadors. Colvin mentions that a sizeable popula-

tion of barn owls quietly inhabits Philadelphia warehouses, flying each evening to nearby wetlands along the Delaware River to feed. When we learn about and grow fond of owl neighbors in our cities, we often find extra incentive to preserve the marshes and streamside habitats they require as foraging areas.

Barn owls are receiving help on several fronts. Progressive federal farm bills promote the setting aside of marginal, easily erodible farmland for conservation purposes. Such conversions of row crops to pastures and meadows favor owls. The Ohio Department of Natural Resources is working with the federal conservation reserve program to establish new foraging areas for barn owls and other grassland species. In addition, the Ohio highway department does not mow roadsides until August, providing about 40,000 acres of grassy rodent habitat for barn owls and their fledglings. In Arkansas, delta ricelands are ideal hunting grounds for barn owls. Erecting nest boxes in these areas appears to be increasing barn owl numbers in the eastern portion of the state.

Farmers who are fortunate enough to entice these birds to their land find that barn owls are better mousetraps than those humans have ever succeeded in designing. These "winged cats" can catch 1,000 or more small rodents for each brood they raise, and in some areas they raise two broods per year. Thus barn owls help limit the numbers of rodents that if left unchecked could damage or consume tons of hay and other grass crops.

Throughout North America, screech owls are the most common raptors in city and suburban habitats. They roost on rock ledges in city parks, in hollow trees, undeveloped woodlots, and cemeteries. Like the barn owl, they conceal themselves by day, thus are unseen by the majority of their human neighbors.

Screech owls prosper on edges where woodlands and meadows meet. They adapt well to rural farmsteads that mix pastures, woods, and orchards. Suburbs with scattered shade trees and dense hedges are also to their liking. They readily accept unpainted wooden nest boxes with openings at least three inches in diameter. Screech owls have also appropriated unused mailboxes and stovepipes in which to raise young.

More than one wood-stove owner has heard strange scratches and rattling sounds inside the firebox in the summer only to open the door and find the inquisitive eyes of a screech owl peering back. The birds sometimes explore too far down the stovepipe and become trapped. One startled acquaintance found a screech owl perched on a lampshade in her living room, where it landed after fluttering down the chimney. The little bird sat patiently as she carried it outside, then it flew away.

In a recent study Frederick R. Gehlback found that suburban screech owls may actually have an easier life than those of rural areas. Typical city owls require only ten to fifteen acres of habitat in comparison to seventy-five acres for rural screech owls. During winter, screech owls dine primarily on rodents and birds the size of house sparrows, juncos, and jays. In warmer months the owls rely more on insects, lizards, small snakes, and frogs. Suburban owls rarely have to leave their own yards to find enough food in the summer. They pounce on earthworms wriggling across wet pavement, snatch moths and katydids from tree branches, and swoop down on crickets and June bugs meandering across the lawn. Urban owlets in Gehlbach's study grew faster and had fewer predators than did their country cousins.

Tawny owls do not seem to mind people nearby. In *Owls of Europe*, Heimo Mikkola recounts the story of a British couple who shared an intimate glimpse into the life of a wild owl that adopted their home as her nest site.

The Lewcocks took into their aviary an orphaned tawny owl, fed her, and later released her when she could fend for herself. During the unusually cold winter over 1978 and 1979, the owl returned frequently and tapped on their window. By spring she was a regular visitor, and when allowed inside, often perched on a wooden cupboard in the dining room. The Lewcocks placed a box lined with grass on the cupboard and in it the owl laid four eggs. Meanwhile, her mate hooted from the garden when he arrived with food but would not enter the house. The female flapped outside to claim her meal, then returned to the nest box. She incubated for a period of thirty days, after which two of the eggs hatched.

Little owls have been associated with human settlements since the days of ancient Greece. In Europe today, these small owls with the scowling expression and bobbing habit are encountered in old parkland and in open country dotted by hedgerows. They may also be observed near cemeteries, orchards, and sports fields. Little owls probably inhabited the British Isles during the Pleistocene Epoch but glaciation drove them

Burrowing owls inhabit underground dens. In Florida, they share suburban housing tracts with human neighbors. (Photo © by Connie Toops)

farther south. A few were reintroduced to southern England in the 1870s, and large numbers of the birds were released around Northamptonshire in the 1890s. They spread throughout much of England, experiencing peak populations in the 1920s and 1930s. Little owl populations in Britain are declining now.

Burrowing owls are unlike other owls in several respects. Social colonies made up of four or five owl families inhabit underground dens. In the American West, where burrowing owls often take over ground squirrel and prairie dog tunnels, the birds repel predators not by hooting but by hissing to imitate a rattlesnake. Since snakes commonly rest in shady burrow entrances, most predators are reluctant to call the owl's bluff. To foil coyotes and badgers, which could smell a nest and dig out the eggs or young birds, burrowing owls collect cow and bison dung. They use the excrement to line the entrance hole, creating a scent screen.

Besides inhabiting western prairies, a separate population of burrowing owls lives in central and southern Florida. Once a vast mosaic of grasses and marshes, the headlands of Florida's St. Johns River and the Kissimmee Prairie provided raised hummocks for owls to nest and plenty of surrounding habitat in which to hunt. Much of this land has now been converted to agriculture or tract housing. Surprisingly, one of the new cities may be home to the largest concentration of nesting raptors in the United States.

Researchers have discovered in the Gulf Coast city of Cape Coral as many as eighty burrowing owls per square mile. The owls are most numerous in a mix of houses and open lots in which no more than three-fifths of the land is developed. Here the owls dig their tunnels, which angle down for twelve to eighteen inches, then run parallel beneath the surface for as much as four feet. Like woodpeckers, their flight is undulating. They drop into the grass from low altitudes to catch mice and frogs. In housing areas, burrowing owls have been seen plucking lizards from patio screens, snapping up beetles on lawns, and capturing moths attracted to porch lights.

Most of their human hosts are very protective of the owls. Many install bird baths and little shade shelters near the burrows in their yards.

Airport runways and golf courses are common locations for burrowing owl colonies. (Photo © by Connie Toops)

Saw-whet owls are one of several species that will seek shelter in wooden nest boxes. (Photo © by Howard Douglas)

One residential lot in the Florida Keys, where another burrowing owl colony is located, has a small sign next to a mound of sandy earth. It reads, "Hoot & Annie, 611½ 10th Street—Do Not Disturb."

The city of Cape Coral adopted the burrowing owl as its mascot. And why not? Burrowing owls are bold enough to tolerate humans watching them from as close as ten feet. At times they seem as curious about us as we are of them. When the young—there can be as many as ten in a brood—finally make their debut from the underground nest, they bow and bob like dancers in a chorus line. The humorous scene captures the hearts of many who have never paid attention to birds before.

Burrowing owls also find the grassy strips along airport runways to their liking. Busy Miami International is a burrowing owl sanctuary, and as a matter of fact, I saw my very first burrowing owl there while coasting along a taxiway in a 727 jet.

Golf courses are favored habitats, but if you are unlucky enough to sink a ball into a burrow, you may never retrieve it. A burrowing owl nest discovered on a Midland, Texas, golf course had a successful brood of owlets plus twenty-seven golf balls the female hoarded into her lair.

While some owls can adjust to urbanization, other species benefit more by placement of nest boxes and platforms in their woodland territories. With increasing use of dying trees for firewood and emphasis on making commercial forests as productive as possible, hollow snags are not as abundant as they once were. Several species of owls will accept unpainted wood boxes in lieu of tree cavities. Others prefer shallow platforms attached to high branches of large trees.

Nest boxes should have small drainage holes in

the floor and be empty except for a few wood chips or sawdust to keep the eggs from rolling. Platforms may be embellished with sticks and twigs to simulate an abandoned raptor nest. Detailed plans, entry hole sizes, and location suggestions for owl species of your area should be available at your nearest wildlife conservation office.

Species that readily use nest boxes include barn, screech, pygmy, little, tawny, Ural, barred, boreal, and saw-whet owls. Great gray and long-eared owls have accepted stick nest platforms. Long-eared and tawny owls are also receptive to wire baskets lined with mosses and grasses attached to the fork of a conifer. Great horned owls will use platforms, and rarely, nest boxes.

Should you become an owl host, do not open the nest box to view the eggs or young. Barn owls will abruptly abandon the area if disturbed while courting, brooding, or raising small chicks. Larger species such as tawny, great horned, and great gray owls will attack with enough force to wound observers or knock them from a ladder. Some years ago Eric Hosking, a British pioneer in the field of bird photography, was watching a tawny owl nest from a nearby blind. The owl caught a glimpse of Hosking's eye glinting through a slit in the blind fabric. Instant-ly she lashed out with her talons, injuring Hosking so severely that he lost sight in that eye.

In Finnish East Lapland bird banders visit the nests of Ural and great gray owls in parties of at least three — one to hold the ladder, one to climb to the nest to band the owlets, and one to act as a lookout. All members wear visored crash helmets because they are frequently attacked, and the owls aim for the banders' heads. The researchers report that heavier great gray owls have a higher success rate of dislodging them from the ladder but Ural owls are more feared because they are more persistent in their defense of the nests.

Nest boxes and platforms alone cannot substitute for adequate habitat, but they are indeed helpful for maintaining some owl populations. In Scandinavia the black woodpecker has declined because of commercial forestry practices. Foresters are, however, beginning to leave islands of trees for them among large cuttings. Birders have put up thousands of nest boxes to compensate for the lack of woodpecker holes in dead and decaying trees. Boreal owls (as well as woodpeckers and tree-nesting ducks) are reaping the benefits. In Holland, barn owls have made a comeback thanks to educational programs and incentives to encourage their access to breeding sites in buildings.

OWL PROWLS

How do owl-watchers locate birds that look like tree stumps during the daytime and move about under cover of darkness? One of the best ways is to find their roosts. A tip-off to an owl roost is the discovery of chalky white washes of excrement on branches or of pellets beneath a tree. If you find such signs, look carefully overhead for a resting owl.

Pellets are a reliable way to discover owls and also to study their food preferences. Owls do not have crops in which to store food. They swallow prey whole and digestion begins soon after. Since owls have relatively weak stomach acids, bones, fur, beaks, feathers, and claws of prey animals are not digested. Rather, hard items accumulate in the gizzard and are regurgitated eight to ten hours after eating. Most owls cast one pellet as the hunting period draws to an end and another several hours after they have gone to roost.

Easily recognized prey remnants such as mammalian jaw bones and bird's beaks are usually contained within owl castings. In the owl's digestive tract, fur and feathers are compressed tightly around a core of sharp bones and claws. When the pellet is finally coughed up, it resembles a felt-covered oval mass, varying in size, shape, and color depending on the species of owl and its diet. For instance, hard black barn owl pellets average 1.9 by 1.0 by 0.8 inches, while tawny owl pellets are gray, crumble easily, and measure about 2.1 by 0.9 by 0.7 inches. Pellets of

tiny saw-whet owls are 0.6 inch in diameter and 1.2 inches long, dense and packed with bones.

Although some might think handling owl pellets would be a nasty experience, all but the freshest casts are firm, dry, and nearly odorless. The pellets decompose slowly, though sometimes you will see evidence that rodents have gnawed on the bones within them. The bones are a source of calcium, and this use by small mammals is an excellent example of nature's recycling plan.

Picking the castings apart with your fingers or tweezers will reveal bones, beaks, fur, and sometimes bits of insect bodies. Many of these remains are identifiable. A bird skull, for instance contains no teeth. Distinctive beak shapes will allow you to determine the bird's family, such as warbler, woodpecker, or finch.

Skulls of mammals are categorized by looking at the size, shape, and arrangement of the teeth. Usually the jaw portions of skulls are undamaged by the owl's digestion, though thinner bones at the back of the head may be crushed. Mice and voles possess wide skulls with two front, chisel-shaped incisor teeth top and bottom. They have molarlike teeth in the rear. Moles and shrews possess elongated skulls with slender teeth used to bite and chew insects. Shrew teeth are tipped with brown. Should you discover a cough ball that is mostly fur with very few bones, it is probably a hawk pellet. The casting of a saw-whet owl may contain only a partial

An owl prowl is an exciting way to meet owls on their own terms. An effective way of locating owls at night is to imitate their calls.(Photo © by Maslowski Wildlife Productions)

Owls cannot digest bones, fur, and other hard items. These items are regurgitated several hours after eating as fur- or feather-wrapped pellets. Pellets scattered on the ground are a tip-off to an owl's roost overhead. (Photo © by Connie Toops)

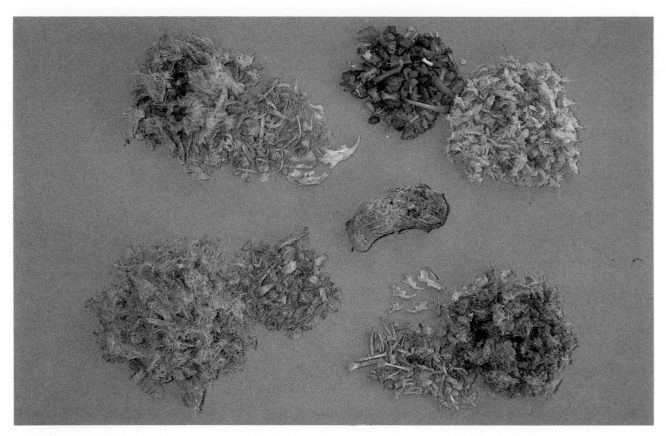

Dissected pellets reveal that this great horned owl's diet consisted primarily of mice. (Photo © by Connie Toops)

skeleton, as these small owls save part of their catch to eat at a later time. In contrast, the pellet of a great horned owl could easily hold the remains of half a dozen mouse-sized animals.

Sometimes the behavior of other birds will reveal the presence of on owl. The antagonistic calls and mobbing actions of crows and jays are worth watching. When these birds band together and scold in one location for a few minutes, there will almost always be a hawk or owl at the focus of their scorn.

Songbirds also band together when they discover an owl. Panicked kinglets and wrens dart from branch to branch, wagging their tails in agitation. Titmice, chickadees, and nuthatches berate the hapless raptor in long, chattering tirades. Sparrows, finches, towhees, even woodpeckers join the fray. Although any species of owl may be lambasted in this manner, saw-whet, screech, and pygmy owls evoke immediate and prolonged wrath.

So deep-seated is this antagonism of songbirds for owls that researchers and enterprising birders put the behavior to use. Birders know that by playing tapes of screech or pygmy owl calls during the daytime, they can entice songbirds into close viewing range. Ornithologist Dwight Smith and his associates, when trying to identify screech owl nest sites, found they could play tape recordings of a screech owl and watch the reactions of local songbirds. If an owl lived in the area and the birds were accustomed to seeing and hearing it around a certain roost, they would immediately begin to mob that roost when they heard the taped call, even if the owl was not present. If owls did not frequent the area, the small birds targeted their wrath on the tape recorder.

Perhaps the most effective way to locate owls

99

Most children are spellbound when they see or hear an owl for the first time. (Photo © by Joe McDonald)

Now at sundown I hear the hooting of an owl, —hoo hoo hoo, hooer hoo. . . . *This is my music each evening.* . . . *It is a sound admirably suited [to] the swamp and to the twilight woods.* . . . *I rejoice that there are owls.* Henry David Thoreau, Journal, November 18, 1851. *(Photo © by Maslowski Wildlife Productions)*

at night is by imitating their calls to elicit a hooted response. More and more people are taking advantage of nighttime opportunities to meet owls on their own terms. Perhaps their first encounter was on a naturalist-guided owl prowl at a park or nature center, but the some procedure can be used in any area.

Transfer onto a cassette tape the recorded voices of owls native to your area. Repeat the call until you have accumulated two to three minutes of sounds for each species. Organize the calls in order of smallest to largest birds.

Before your field trip, put fresh batteries in the tape player and in your flashlight. Covering the light source with red cellophane will dim the beam so it is not as frightening to the owls. Since midwinter to early spring are the times owls are most vocal, dress warmly. If you think that being out late in a particular area could arouse suspicion, call ahead to local police, park rangers, or other law enforcement authorities to explain what you will be doing.

Windless nights are best for owl prowls because sounds carry better and are easier to pinpoint. Full or partial moonlight is helpful for spotting the birds. Plan a walking or driving route with pauses at the edges of forests, marshes, and streams. At each stop, set the tape player at midvolume and broadcast the recordings. Listen for a few moments between species. When an owl is within earshot, it will usually return a call almost immediately. If the tapes don't garner a response, move to another location and try again.

If you are in or near an owl's territory when you play its call, the bird may fly quite close to investigate. Owls often arrive noiselessly. Be very still until you pinpoint their location. Sometimes it is possible to beam your flashlight on the bird for a moment to study it.

One night a naturalist friend at Everglades Na-

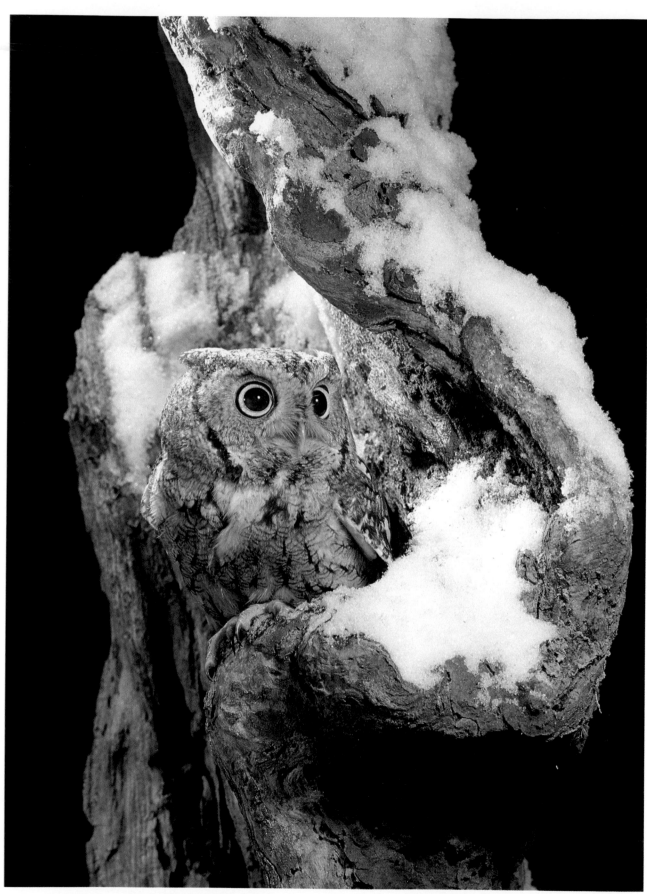

Owls are most vocal in middle to late winter when they are establishing territories. Windless nights are best for owl prowls because sounds carry better. (Photo © by Maslowski Wildlife Productions)

tional Park inadvertently invited a pair of barred owls to his outdoor evening program. He showed a film that included a recorded barred owl call. As the film rolled on, he heard more calls, but they were not in synch with the movie. Thinking quickly, he stopped the film and switched on the amphitheater lights. There, above the screen next to the loudspeaker, sat a pair of barred owls. They nodded, bowed, and *who-all*ed to reinforce their ownership of the territory as a fascinated audience watched. With wings half-spread and heads twisting first left, then right, they uttered chuckles and maniacal laughter. Then the owls consummated their display by mating. They finally flew away to the applause of delighted park visitors.

Be aware that using a tape recording to lure an owl close does invade a delicately balanced realm of bird offense and defense. Avian owners of a territory instinctively call louder and longer than an invader. If the invader persists, the owner may eventually fall silent, or in the worst case, be overwhelmed and driven from its own home range. A human operating a tape recorder may not appreciate how easy it is to broadcast the sound in comparison to the energy expended by and stress factors imposed on the responding owl. Taped calls should be used sparingly — only to catch a glimpse of the bird and never so long as to irritate other birds or birders in the area. If you are planning an owl prowl in a park or preserve, check to see whether the use of tapes is allowed.

For unusual species, such as ferruginous pygmy owls and elf owls that sometimes inhabit heavily birded locales in southern Texas and Arizona, specific directions to a particular roost may be given by rare bird alert networks. While each individual watcher may only play tapes a short time, the cumulative effect of observers rousing a bird night after night may drive it away or deprive it of necessary hunting time. It is best not to call rare birds with tapes.

One enjoyable alternative to using taped calls is learning to imitate owls with your own voice. Several naturalists in my acquaintance do good enough impressions of barred, great horned, and screech owls to make me reach for my binoculars. An advantage of learning to hoot is that you can go owling any time without worrying about taking a tape player. Secondly, there is less chance of overtaxing the responding owl because your voice may wear out sooner than its will.

Listen to recordings at home and try to imitate the pitch and sound patterns. Don Hall, an expert owl caller, passes along these tips for replicating the quavering whistle of a screech owl: Wet your whistle by concentrating saliva on the back of your tongue. Then tilt your head back and whistle gently, letting the saliva bubble.

There is nothing more warming on a winter night, when the chill has penetrated down jackets and wool mittens, than to softly imitate the call of a screech owl and have it returned by the real thing. If you enjoy such outings, take your children or those of friends. Introduce them to these enchanting creatures of the night. Even the wiggliest kids will freeze in their tracks and listen in awe to the eerie, tremulous call of an owl.

Impaired owls can contribute to wildlife conservation. Captive owls will court, mate, and raise chicks that can be released into the wild. (Photo © by Connie Toops)

OWLS AS EDUCATORS

Who-who-who-whoo, hooted David Livingston, animal program coordinator at Brukner Nature Center near Troy, Ohio, as he opened the plywood door of an owl cage. *Who-who-who-whooaah*, came a reply from inside. Bernice, a female barred owl turned expectantly toward the sound of David's voice, her white throat puffing comically with each hoot.

"Bernice has been with us for several years," Livingston explained. "She's blind, but I think she recognizes my voice," he continued. "She's so gentle I don't even need gloves when I pick her up."

"She loves to have her head scratched," David said as he placed the large bird on a perch. I obliged, my fingers disappearing nearly half their length into her fluffy ruff of feathers before I felt and scratched her head.

As my behind-the-scenes tour continued, David explained that Bernice stays at the center on a long-term educational permit issued by the U.S. Fish and Wildlife Service. Although she will never be released into the wild, she is a valuable asset in programs at the center as well as traveling with David to area schools. On the wall behind Bernice's abode was a row of cages where several injured birds of prey were recuperating. Their stay here would be short, and once healed, they would return to nature.

Brukner is typical of the approximately five hundred raptor treatment centers in the United States. Although a few of the larger ones are associated with zoos, wildlife refuges, or medical research facilities, most are privately funded and rely heavily on volunteers. Caregivers are regulated by federal permits, with some states requiring additional licensing.

Coordinators at most raptor centers report their patient loads have increased during the past decade. As human habitation expands into the once-wild countryside, native animals are more likely to encounter our vehicles, machinery, and poisons. It is not unusual for some of the larger centers to treat several hundred raptors annually.

According to Ed Clark, director of the Wildlife Center of Virginia, collisions with autos account for a high percentage of owl injuries. Of the owls struck by autos that Clark receives, 95 percent are injured on the left side. He theorizes that owls hunting along a roadside see prey crossing the highway. They fly in from behind and are struck by oncoming vehicles in the near lane.

Owls tangled in fences and fishing line, birds that collide with buildings, victims of poisoning, and those illegally shot or trapped account for the majority of other owl injuries. Many are first-year birds not yet familiar with avoiding human obstacles and dangers. A few of them are simply hungry because they haven't mastered prey-catching well enough.

If you should ever find a bedraggled, helpless raptor, the best action is to move it quickly to a rehabilitation center. Call your local game warden if you are unsure where to take the bird. It is illegal to keep or try to treat these birds yourself. Any delays in seeking professional help for injured wildlife reduce their chances for survival.

Approach the bird from behind to avoid being struck by sharp beak or talons. Drape a light towel or sheet over the bird, anticipating that it may panic and struggle at first. Restrain it as soon

David Livingston greets Bernice, a blind barred owl used in educational programs at Brukner Nature Center. (Photo © by Connie Toops)

David Livingston exercises an imprinted barn owl used in educational programs at Brukner Nature Center. (Photo © by Connie Toops)

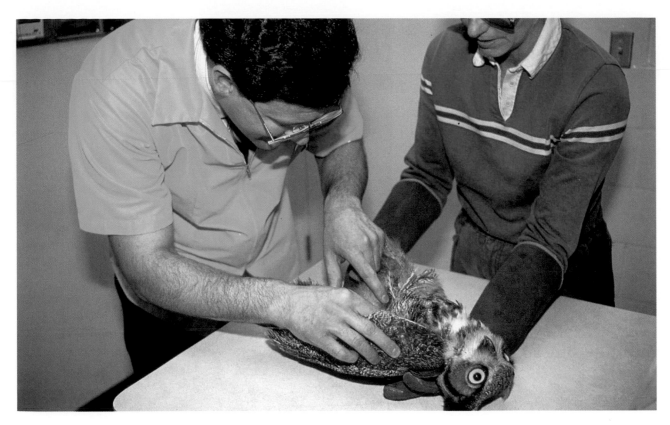

Veterinarian Michael Brown treats a great horned owl that became entangled in a barbed wire fence. Swift transport to a raptor rehabilitation center increases the chances of survival for injured owls. (Photo © by Ralph Ramey)

as possible. As you gather it up in the covering, be sure wings fold in against the bird's body. Transfer the injured raptor to a ventilated cardboard box only slightly larger than the bird. Remove the towel or sheet so the raptor does not overheat, and close the box securely. It is not necessary to provide food or water. Write down as much information as possible about the situation in which the bird was discovered so rehabilitators can release it in its home territory after treatment.

Veterinarians' knowledge of how to tend raptors has increased tremendously during the past decade. According to Dr. Gary Duke, founder of the Raptor Center at the University of Minnesota's College of Veterinary Medicine, staff members feel a sense of accomplishment each time an individual bird is rehabilitated. He continues that an even more important contribution of these

programs is the futhering of research, examination, and treatment procedures. At veterinary hospitals such as the Raptor Center, it has now become routine to splint and surgically pin broken bones, medicate infections, and supplement the diets of ailing birds with vitamins. At most centers the less severely injured birds can usually be released in three to ten weeks. Others may be kept through periods of inclement weather or until they can once again hunt with ease. These birds are usually housed in secluded cages away from people to reduce stress and familiarity with humans.

Over the past few years many rehabilitation centers have achieved release rates of about 50 percent. Sometimes when they return a bird to the site where it was found, rehabilitators witness a joyous mate greeting the releasee.

A significant number of the birds treated at raptor centers, however, have injuries that prevent their return to the wild. Gunshot wounds may shatter delicate wing bones, requiring immobilization or removal of a portion of the wing. Collisions frequently leave owls blinded in one or both eyes. When the birds are obviously suffering from their injuries, they are euthanized. But about one-quarter of the raptors received and treated are able to live long and useful lives in at the raptor centers or in zoos.

In captivity, where food is plentiful and the rigors of competing for a territory are not a concern, owls enjoy lengthy lifespans. Combined records for Europe and North America place the oldest known captive owls and their ages as follows: great gray, forty; great horned, thirty-eight; snowy, thirty-five; tawny, twenty-seven; barred, twenty-three; and barn, twenty-one years.

Banding studies indicate, however, that most wild owls do not approach these ages. Banding, or ringing, the legs of birds to obtain scientific information originated in Germany in the 1740s. At that time small pieces of parchment were tied to the legs of swallows. Finders were asked to report where the birds spent the winter. Today numbered aluminum bands are used by ornithologists who record the species, sex, and age of the bird, as well as when and where it is banded. As of 1989, more than 40 million band numbers have been entered in computer files of the U.S. Fish and Wildlife Service Bird Banding Lab.

Band returns from killed, injured, or recaptured owls increase ornithologist's knowledge about where these birds travel and how long they live. The percentage of band returns for owls is low, probably because many are secretive, solitary birds that seldom leave their home territories. From combined returns for the Northern Hemisphere, the longest-lived wild owls and their ages in years are: long-eared, twenty-seven; eagle and barn, twenty-one; great horned, nineteen; tawny and barred, eighteen; Ural, fourteen; screech, thirteen; short-eared, twelve; snowy and scops, ten.

Even these records are potentially misleading. The percentage of immature birds received at raptor treatment centers indicates that perhaps half of the owls born each spring do not survive their first year. In the wild a three-year-old barn

owl and a five-year-old great gray would be nearing the end of their expected lives.

Great horned, screech, and barred owls, the most numerous species encountered at United States treatment centers, often adapt well to educational programs. Some of the birds remain on permanent display in cages at nature centers and zoos. Many more possess the temperament and trust to allow themselves to be used in environmental education programs. Through such encounters, Ed Clark estimates the Wildlife Center of Virginia and its satellite birds of prey program at Shenandoah National Park reach about 50,000 people annually with positive information about raptors and their role in our world. Each year David Hitzig, director of education for the Tropical Audubon Society, offers raptor awareness programs for some 32,000 school children in metropolitan Miami, Florida.

One of the most unusual educational programs is the Raptory Theatre, associated with the Raptor Rehabilitation and Propagation Project (RRPP) in Eureka, Missouri. A trained entourage of naturalists, hawks, and owls travels to zoos throughout the country presenting entertaining programs about birds of prey. At the opposite end of the spectrum, the Vermont Raptor Center in Woodstock, Vermont, displays nonreleasable birds in huge cages that depict their native habitats. The intent of such informative displays is to allow people to see how beautiful and special raptors are. Through such experiences, we may better understand some of the threats raptors face worldwide.

Many centers, including the Raptor Center, RRPP, Wildlife Center of Virginia, and Florida Audubon Society's Center for Birds of Prey, offer internships. These programs allow high school and college students to gain practical experience in the relatively new field of raptor rehabilitation. The Wildlife Center of Virginia, the largest professionally staffed and equipped veterinary hospital for wild animals in the world, conducts cooperative programs with six univer-

Eagle owls have been used in captive breeding programs that bolster wild populations of the European species. (Photo © by Bill Hartman)

Motor vehicle accidents account for the majority of owl injuries and deaths. (Photo © by Richard Smith)

Permanently disabled owls are frequently used in educational encounters at schools and parks. In this photo, sixth graders meet an imprinted barred owl at the Glen Helen Outdoor Center, Yellow Springs, Ohio. (Photo © by Ralph Ramey)

sities. The center also welcomes practicing vets who wish to increase their skills in the care of wild creatures, a specialty not included in most regular college classes. Medical experience in treating pesticide poisoning or performing surgery on injured birds, gained here and at other veterinary research facilities such as the University of Minnesota's Raptor Center, is resulting in much higher release rates than ever dreamed of. Some of this knowledge also benefits endangered species recovery programs.

Owls that may never fly free can still make significant contributions. For a quarter-century Kay McKeever of the Owl Rehabilitation Research Foundation in Vineland Station, Ontario, has been using permanently damaged wild birds to study owl behavior and interpersonal relationships. McKeever keeps some 140 owls in big flight enclosures at the center, located on the narrow arm of land that separates Lake Erie and Lake Ontario. The large cages are designed to accommodate six owls, and although the cages are connected by overhead flyways, each owl has a place to which it can retreat for privacy. Three males and three females of the same species are placed in each compound. Observers note their behavior by watching closed-circuit television.

McKeever has learned that nonmigratory owls, such as screech and great horned, have strong bonds with their mates throughout the year. Outside of the nesting period, however, each bird of the mated pair must have its own separate space. Migrant species, including saw-whet, burrowing, and flammulated owls, return to a specific place each year rather than to the same mate. Outside of the breeding season, these owls are not with each other in the wild. When caged, they fight. The females, McKeever has learned, are the most aggressive. In order for these owls to breed in captivity, they cannot be housed together year-round.

McKeever also studies the reactions of owls that have lost life-long mates. She reports that great horned and great gray owls in her care have taken from three to seven years to relinquish bonds with old mates and form breeding attachments with replacements.

Many owls at the Owl Rehabilitation Research Foundation mate and raise chicks. Once youngsters learn to hunt live mice in conditions simulating what they will encounter in the wild, they are released into proper habitats. McKeever has proven that if captive owls feel comfortable in their surroundings and pairs receive the proper stimuli, they will breed or at least raise foster chicks. As in the wild, courtship begins with the male owl hooting. The couple performs mutual preening, and soon after the female may lay eggs. Several years ago, almost by accident, the staff at the Florida Audubon's Center for Birds of Prey discovered one of their great horned owls had strong foster parenting instincts.

The owl was an abnormally imprinted male. It was raised by well-meaning, but uninformed, private citizens who allowed the owl to make the unnatural association that humans are friends. A young owl, like most baby birds, will follow and imitate the first large creature that feeds and pays attention to it. Visual imprinting occurs from the time the chick can focus its eyes clearly (about ten days after hatching for a great horned owl) until it leaves the parents and begins to feed on its own. Birds, imprinted on humans though not physically impaired, are generally not released because their psychological confusion keeps them from breeding. Long ago that might not have been a concern, but now with habitat becoming scarce in many areas, most rehabilitators feel such imprinted birds should not take up wild space that could be used by normally reproducing birds.

The imprinted Florida owl tried to court the human staff rather than the female in his cage. The female, however, was stimulated by his courting calls and laid several unfertilized eggs. The male, in a role unknown in nature, pushed her off the nest and took over incubation. Of course the infertile eggs did not hatch, but by that time the center was receiving its usual springtime number of orphaned baby birds. One of the staff members substituted a two-week-old

111

In captivity, owls are fed surplus lab rodents or mice and rats raised especially for them. Where food is plentiful and predators absent, owls enjoy long lives. The oldest great horned owl known lived thirty-eight years. (Photo © by Connie Toops)

owlet for the eggs, and the imprinted owl chirped excitedly.

"Mr. Mom," as the owl became known to his keepers, tenderly offered food to his adopted baby. As more orphaned great horned chicks were brought to the center, "Mr. Mom" also took them under his wing. All the keepers had to do was provide plenty of mice. The foster parent kept the chicks fed, and later when the chicks were old enough, the owls all moved to a flight cage where "Mr. Mom" showed the babies how to pounce on live prey. Eventually all of the fledglings were released into the wild.

Permanently injured barn and burrowing owls, both of which have dwindling populations in the wild, breed prolifically in captivity. Once the juvenile birds are old enough to hunt on their own, they can be released to bolster remaining natural populations.

Chick rescue calls keep rehabilitation staffers busy throughout the spring and early summer. Sometimes residents cut down a tree before realizing it contains an owl den. They also find frisky owlets that have jumped from the nest before they can fly. The ideal solution is to return the chicks to their own home, or if it cannot be found, to a nearby nest of the same species. Owls can't count, and usually an extra chick or two will not be noticed. Placing young owls back in a nest should never be attempted without first consulting rehabilitators or state game officials. In many cases irate owl parents will dive-bomb well-meaning rescuers.

If an orphan cannot be placed with wild parents or captive foster owls, rehabilitators feed it using an owl puppet so it will not imprint on humans. Caged owls of the same species may be placed nearby to attract the young bird's attention for imprinting. When a juvenile is old enough to begin hunting on its own, it is placed in a "hacking" cage atop a pole in the wild. This falconer's technique allows young birds to look over the release site while still having food provided regularly at the cage. Once the

juveniles are capable of flight, the cage door is opened. The youngsters become bolder and better hunters with age and will finally ignore the hacking cage. Hacked owls often return to that general vicinity as adults to claim a territory.

Wildlife rehabilitation is a controversial subject. Some biologists contend that for all the money spent on treating, housing, and feeding injured raptors, little is done to augment wild populations. "Wouldn't the money be better spent on habitat preservation?" detractors query.

Rehabilitation is costly, but people involved in these programs argue that it offers a very personal way to express human concern about wildlife. They also cite the fact that most injuries result from human obstacles and interference. Collisions with autos and plate glass windows, gunshot wounds, and power line burns are not natural consequences. "That's what makes education so important," states David Hitzig of Miami's Tropical Audubon Society. He emphasizes that many of these accidents are direct results of humans developing land that was once wild. "Not only do we want to fix the injuries," Hitzig continues, "but we want to teach people how to prevent them in the future."

"Human-caused problems are easier to fix," adds Gary Duke, "than natural problems like disease and predation."

Wildlife rehabilitators — many of whom donate their time and expertise — feel that their efforts help in a small way to make up for constraints inflicted by humankind on wild creatures. Overwhelming positive reactions to displays and programs sponsored by rehabilitation centers have demonstrated that the more urbanized the human race becomes, the more we seem to long for contact with wild creatures. If exposing people to raptors in general, and owls in particular, can end the historic prejudices against these birds of prey and develop within us an awareness of their importance in the natural scheme, such programs are definitely serving a useful purpose.

Spotted Owl Habitat: *Quiet, old-growth forests of the Pacific Northwest are home to a dwindling number of northern spotted owls. Centuries-old Douglas firs, Sitka spruces, western red cedars, and western hemlocks dwarf the vine maples and delicate wildflowers that grow on the shady forest floor. Only 2 percent of this virgin old-growth forest remains.* (Photo © by Pat Toops)

Spotted Owl Habitat: *Spotted owls are sedate in comparison to other owls. They remain in the same home range with the same mate year after year. Spotted owls do not breed until three years of age and they lay an average of only two eggs. (Photo © by Norman Barrett)*

Spotted Owl Habitat: *Male spotted owls court females by presenting food to them, but spotted owls do not nest every year. They seem to abandon their reproductive attempts when food is scarce. In years when spotted owls do raise offspring, the young birds beg food from their parents until fall. Then the juveniles temporarily join loose flocks of other unmated spotted owls until it is time to establish their own nesting territories. (Photo © by Norman Barrett, courtesy USDA Forest Service)*

Spotted Owl Habitat: *In 1990, Pacific old-growth forests were disappearing at the rate of 1.5 square miles per week. Continued intensive logging could destroy half of the spotted owls' habitat within the next few years. The mortality of young spotted owls is extremely high, and scientists believe a major reason is that the young birds have little new habitat in which to expand. (Photo © by Connie Toops)*

117

Despite the spread of agriculture and urbanization, many owls continue to find suitable places to hunt and raise young. Their future, however, is dependent upon coexistence with humans. (Photo © by Maslowski Wildlife Productions)

WHAT LIES AHEAD?

The countryside in both Europe and North America is very different today than it was thousands of years ago. Forests and wetlands have dwindled, replaced here by cities and there by agrarian landscapes. The plow and the bulldozer have eliminated native plants, replacing them with pavement and monocultured crops. Yet amid the suburbs, some woodlots survive, and beyond the corporate limits lie forested tracts. Despite clearing and draining, owls have continued to find places to hunt and to raise their young. Their future, however, is increasingly dependent upon coexistence with human beings.

Although many owls live within parks and preserves, far greater numbers reside on private land. While smaller owls may naturally fall prey to hawks and other owls, large owls have people as their main nemesis. Fortunately, increasing numbers of foresters and landowners are beginning to recognize the value of owls and are managing their acreages to include the forest types, edge effects, and mature stands that benefit birds of prey. In forests where trees are harvested before they become ideal for owl nests, some managers encourage owls to remain by erecting nesting boxes or baskets. Increases in Ural and boreal owl populations in Europe are direct results of such conservation efforts.

Great gray owls have accepted artificial stick-nest platforms where hollow snags are scarce in the northern United States, Canada, and Scandinavia. Great gray owl numbers are stable in northern North America and Europe, but they are declining at the southern edge of their range in the United States. These losses seem to be linked with widespread logging and conversion of forests to grazing lands. In California great gray owls are in danger. Only fifty birds remain, about half of which live within Yosemite National Park.

Supplying owls with nest boxes can temporarily bolster their numbers, but artificial nests are no substitute for ample habitat. The question of habitat preservation, which ultimately governs long-term owl survival, is most poignant as it relates to the plight of the spotted owl in the Pacific Northwest.

Complications always arise when humans compete with wildlife for the same land. Although spotted owls will occasionally nest in second growth, they usually require large, undisturbed tracts of virgin forest. Spotted owls once lived throughout the Pacific Northwest, but with commercial cutting of much of the privately owned old timber, most remaining populations are found within the boundaries of federal forests and national parks.

The timber industry is a major force in the economy of this region, and to a logger, virgin forests represent hundreds of jobs and thousands of dollars in revenues. Lumber interests feel they are entitled to harvest the "overmature" (as old growth is classified) timber on U.S. Forest Service and Bureau of Land Management lands.

One problem, however, is that logging divides the large tracts necessary for spotted owls into islands of trees surrounded by expansive clearcuts.

Environmentalists and timber interests are working to determine how much fragmentation of this forest habitat the owls can withstand. The U.S. Forest Service selected the spotted owl as an "indicator species," a representative animal used to measure the health and integrity of old-growth forests. From a naturalist's view, there are a thousand reasons to protect these tracts, including the preservation of Vaux's swifts and marbled murrelets, which also nest in huge hollow snags. But the owl with the soulful brown eyes has gained the most notoriety. It has become embodied in a bitter regional controversy, emerging as a symbol of the global problem of vanishing forests. Although spotted owls were previously recognized by Oregon and Washington as a species of environmental concern, they were not declared federally threatened until 1990. This decision closes more old-growth stands to logging, a move that has wide economic and environmental repercussions. Several years earlier, in protest of owl conservation blocking jobs and timber profits, two spotted owls were bludgeoned to death by anti-preservationists on the Olympic Peninsula. Local bumper stickers and baseball caps carry mottos such as "I like spotted owls — FRIED" and "Save a logger, kill a spotted owl." Such reactionary attitudes make conservationists even more determined to defend the owls and their environs.

Sitting quietly in the mossy forests, as their ancestors have for generations, are the 2,000 or so remaining pairs of spotted owls. In the controversy centered on them, two things are certain. Spotted owls cannot prosper without old-growth forests, and a logged area takes a minimum of two hundred years to recover to satisfactory owl habitat. If the last large tracts are cut, spotted owls have little chance except in small, isolated preserves. Under such conditions there may not be enough genetic diversity for the owls to survive.

In addition, barred owls have been steadily colonizing westward for decades. As generalists in food and habitat requirements, they are successfully using the increasing edge habitat, where harvesting of timber, grazing, and other forms of human land management have carved into once-vast forests. In the Pacific Northwest, barred owls are expanding their range at the expense of less aggressive spotted owls.

Elsewhere, hawk owls and long-eared owls are believed to be decreasing throughout the Northern Hemisphere, though their choice of remote habitats and their secretive ways make them difficult to study. In Europe, limited captive breeding and release programs have helped combat declines in eagle owl populations. More important, however, have been active educational programs emphasizing owl conservation, passage of laws protecting all owls, and special protection status given to critical species, such as barn and snowy owls.

Barn owls adapt readily to properly installed nest boxes but are not able to reproduce successfully unless they have adequate grassland hunting territories nearby. They are endangered throughout a significant part of their North American range and are of increasing concern in much of Europe. As in the American Midwest, barn owl populations are dwindling in the southeastern part of Britain, where barn owls were once quite common. Old hollow elms in which they nested have been cut and open-plan barns replaced by modern, weather-tight buildings. Intensive agricultural practices emphasizing row crops have converted grassy meadows into tilled fields. Urban sprawl has eliminated additional habitat. The Royal Society for the Protection of Birds is encouraging barn owl conservation through an educational program and placement of nest boxes.

The management strategy for barn owls differs from that for most other raptors. Eagles and peregrine falcons, for instance, must reach their fourth or fifth year before they mate and lay eggs. Barn owls are short-lived in the wild but during their typical two- or three-year life spans, they have an amazingly high reproductive capability if they have access to adequate prey.

Barn owl researcher Bruce Colvin calls barn

Although nest boxes supplement the loss of hollow trees for some species, the key to long-term owl survival is preservation of quality habitat. (Photo © by Pat Toops)

owls "reproductive machines," comparing their fecundity to that of rabbits. Capable of first breeding at seven months old, laying up to ten eggs per nesting (although six offspring per brood is more normal), and raising two broods in some years, barn owls demonstrate prolific potential for colonization of favorable habitats. Habitat, Colvin asserts, is the bellwether of barn owl survival.

Burrowing owls are vanishing from their range in the western United States, a direct result of conversion of grasslands to irrigated agricultural fields. The process displaces prairie dogs and badgers, thus destroys homes and hunting areas suitable for the owls. In Florida burrowing owls are moving onto new sites with the spread of suburbia, but they are still considered a "species of special concern." Suburban burrowing owls do not prosper in areas with less than 40 percent open space. For many housing developers, this much unused space is considered "wasted" space. But when burrowing owls can-

not find enough grassland in which to feed or when they encounter neighborhood pets, cars, or vandals too frequently, they disappear from the cityscape.

Human manipulation of habitat affects other owls, but with less grave consequences. Tawny owls breed as successfully in numerous city parks, gardens, and woodlots as in their original deep forest haunts. Screech owls may not find as many hollow trees in the woodlands and along streams as they once did, but where nest sites are available, they adapt well to areas around rural and suburban dwellings.

The fact that most owls eat rodents has led many humans to regard them as valuable. This diet has also helped owls avoid the eggshell thinning problems experienced by eagles and ospreys. These raptors ingest chlorinated hydrocarbons (such as DDT) concentrated in the fish they eat.

121

Barred owls, which are better suited to life in second-growth forests, have expanded their range in the Pacific Northwest at the expense of spotted owls. (Photo © by Maslowski Wildlife Productions)

Although rodents may be abundant in recently cleared woodlands, great gray owls are unable to take advantage of this prey unless they have enough perches nearby to use as listening posts. (Photo © by Michael Quinton)

Boreal owls, especially in Scandinavia, have benefited from the placement of nest boxes in areas where timber has been harvested. (Photo © by Gary Meszaros)

For the ferruginous pygmy owl, small size and secretive habits are protection from human disruption. In recent years we have come to recognize the vital environmental role that owls play in maintaining the balance of nature. (Photo © by Robert Behrstock)

The pesticides are directly linked with low reproduction of eagle and osprey chicks. In countries where such pesticides have been banned, raptor numbers are increasing. The dangerous pesticides are still used, however, in many Third World nations.

As raptors, owls occupy a position near the top of the food chain, and in so doing, they serve as valuable barometers of environmental health. If there is trouble—such as a pesticide poisoning—that could eventually affect the health of human beings, changes in owl populations may reflect these imbalances while there is still time to correct them.

The secretive nighttime habits of many owls make them less likely to be disturbed by humans, although this does not protect owls from collisions with motor vehicles. Education about the owl's important ecological role has led to a decline in the number of birds intentionally shot and trapped, but despite their illegality these activities still occur. Minimizing disruptions of nesting owls is another key to their successful conservation.

Rather than regarding owls as creatures of the dark side, as spirit demons and objects of fear, we now know them as beautiful, specialized hunters, vital to the balance of nature. We take pleasure in watching owls—the wonder of their noiseless flight and the quickness of their senses. Perhaps we are finally learning there is more reward in observing and practicing stewardship of nature than in trying to triumph over it.

Imagining a world without owls is akin to imagining nightfall without the emergence of twinkling stars. Yes, the human race could probably survive without distant stars or neighboring owls. But the awe and wonder both give to the evening hours make us all the richer for experiencing them.

Barn owl numbers are dwindling as wet meadows and other suitable grasslands are converted to row crops or suburbia. (Photo © by Maslowski Wildlife Productions)

LIST OF OWL SPECIES

REFERENCES

Barrett, Norman M. "The Spotted Owl." *Bird Watcher's Digest* 12 (Sept. 1989): 52–57.

Bent, Arthur C. *Life Histories of North American Birds of Prey.* New York: Dover, 1961.

Bergman, Charles A. "Flaming Owl of the Ponderosa." *Audubon* 85 (Nov. 1983): 66–71.

Bergman, Charles A. "Face-to-Face with the Stalwart Imp of Cactus Country." *Smithsonian* (Dec. 1984): 123–131.

Bergman, Charles A. "Invaders from the Far North." *National Wildlife* 25 (Oct. 1985): 34–39.

Bull, Evelyn L. and Mark G. Henjum. "The Social Great Gray Owl." *Bird Watcher's Digest* 11 (Sept. 1988): 68–75.

Gehlbach, Frederick R. "Odd Couples of Suburbia." *Natural History* 95 (June 1986): 56–64.

Green, Gregory A. "Living on Borrowed Turf." *Natural History* 97 (Sept. 1988): 58–65.

Hall, Don Alan. "Quarvering and Tootling Owls." *Birder's World* 3 (Oct. 1989): 10–13.

Heintzelman, Donald S. *Guide to Owl Watching in North America.* Piscataway, NJ: Winchester Press, 1984.

Holmgren, Virginia C. *Owls in Folklore and Natural History.* Santa Barbara, CA: Capra Press, 1988.

Jenkins, Tom. "Raptor Rescue." *Birder's World* 3 (Dec. 1989): 26–29.

Johnsgard, Paul A. *North American Owls: Biology and Natural History.* Washington, DC: Smithsonian Institution Press, 1988.

Kerlinger, Paul, and M. Ross Lein. "Population Ecology of Snowy Owls During Winter on the Great Plains of North America." *The Condor* 90 (1988): 866–874.

Laycock, George: "Dark Days for Barn Owls." *Audubon* 87 (Nov. 1985): 28–31.

Mikkola, Heimo. *Owls of Europe.* Vermilion, SD: Buteo Books, 1983.

Mooney, Rick. "Helping a Heartland Hunter." *National Wildlife* 26 (June 1988): 40–44.

Nero, Robert W. "Denizen of the Northern Forests." *Birder's World* 2 (Sept. 1988): 20–25.

Nero, Robert W. *The Great Gray Owl: Phantom of the Northern Forest.* Washington, DC: Smithsonian Institution Press, 1980.

Perrins, Christopher. *New Generation Guide to the Birds of Britain and Europe.* Austin, TX: University of Texas Press, 1987.

Quinton, Michael S. *Ghost of the Forest: The Great Gray Owl.* Flagstaff, ND: Northland Press, 1988.

Rowe, M. P., T. Wesemon, and A. Sisson. "Burrowing Owls in Florida's Urban Underground." *Bird Watcher's Digest* 10 (Sept. 1987): 17–21.

Rowe, Matthew. "The Owl that Traded a Hoot for a Hiss." *Natural History* 98 (May 1989): 32–33.

Sayre, Roxanna. "An Invasion to Remember." *Audubon* 82 (Jan. 1980): 52–55.

Scott, Jack Denton. "Bubo Rules the Night." *National Wildlife* 11 (Dec. 1973): 24–27.

Smith, Dwight G., Arnold Devine, and Ray Gilbert. "Screech Owl Roost Site Selection." *Birding* 19 (Aug. 1987): 6–15.

Stefferud, Alfred, ed. *Birds in Our Lives.* Washington, DC: U.S. Government Printing Office, 1966.

Stokes, Donald, and L. Stokes. "Why are Female Hawks Larger than Males?" *Bird Watcher's Digest* 10 (Sept. 1987): 77.

Trapp, Douglas E. "The Not So Common Barn Owl." *Bird Watcher's Digest* 12 (Sept. 1989): 32–37.

Tucker, Jim. "Basic Birding: Using Tape Recorders." *Birding* 17 (Aug. 1985): 159–160.

Tuttle, Liza. "End of the Old-Growth Canopy." *National Parks* 61 (May 1987): 16–21.

Wennerstrom, Jack. "Crows and Raptors." *Bird Watcher's Digest* 11 (Sept. 1988): 80–83.

Wolfe, Art. "Long-eared Owls, Masters of the Night." *National Geographic* 157 (June 1980): 30–35.

Wotton, Michael. "Summer of the White Owl." *Audubon* 78 (July 1976): 32–41.

Over: Though slightly smaller than a robin, the saw-whet owl is an efficient and aggressive hunter. (Photo © by Breck Kent)